QUEEN VICTORIA
IS VERY ILL

QUEEN VICTORIA IS VERY ILL

a memoir by
Katharine Moore

Allison & Busby
Published by W.H. Allen & Co. Plc

An Allison & Busby book
Published in 1988 by
W.H. Allen & Co. Plc
44 Hill Street
London W1X 8LB

Printed and bound in Great Britain by
Mackays of Chatham Ltd, Chatham, Kent

ISBN 0 85031 910 2

CONTENTS

CONTENTS

To my grandchildren

CHAPTER ONE

1901–1903
The century and I are very young together

'Queen Victoria is very ill, you must ask God to make her better,' said my father. I was saying my evening prayers, kneeling up in my cot. All round my cot were little black iron knobs which, as soon as I was left alone, turned into little black boys but I was not afraid of them, I rather liked them. *Little Black Sambo* was my favourite book and I knew it by heart. Besides, they were kept in order by the four bigger brass boys at the corners.

'Please God make the Queen well,' I said. But she died and everyone wore black clothes or black bands round their arms. I was interested but unmoved and, when told a short time after to pray for an aunt who was ill, I shook my head and said, 'The Queen is dead.' My aunt however recovered without my prayers.

The numinous was very real to me. First, there were God and Jesus who roughly corresponded to my father and mother. God and my father were all powerful and all knowing: they gave orders and had to be obeyed; sometimes they shouted. My father could not shout so loudly as God when it thundered, but he had a good try. Jesus and my mother never shouted and they loved me whatever I did, though they too liked to be obeyed. Jesus had the advantage over my mother in being always there. In the night, whenever I had to get out of my safe bed, I whispered 'Jesus, Jesus.' It stopped the furniture from pouncing on me in the dark.

I enjoyed life but I was frightened of many things – the poplar trees down the road that never stopped talking to

9

themselves, the field beyond our garden gate which was alien ground, the hot water cistern, and the Devil. I had bad dreams; horses were always pursuing me but I got to know that if I lay down bravely and let them gallop over me, it didn't hurt. The worst dream I ever had in my life was before I was six years old. I know this because we moved home when I was five and a half and I had this dream in the old house. I was in the High Street in Reigate, the Surrey market town not far from where we lived, and I had lost my mother. There were people all round me and they said, 'We know where she is, we'll take you to her.' I did not trust them but I went with them for I did not see what else I could do. They began to laugh at me and their faces were mocking. They led me to Mrs Davis's linen draper's shop where I had often been with my mother and there she was sitting on the high bentwood chair at the counter. I ran up to her full of joy and took her gloved hand in mine – but it was cold and stuffed and I knew she was dead.

I did not know anything about death except that it had happened to Queen Victoria and our fat fox terrier Jack, so I can only account for this dream by some atavistic memory or from the influence of the Bible stories that my father told me every morning when I was allowed to come into the big brass double bed beside my cot. I liked the stories but I liked it better when my father had gone to have his cold bath and I had my mother to myself, and it was when I was luxuriating in this one morning that my two sisters and my brother burst into the room and said solemnly 'Jack is dead.' I hadn't loved Jack and I was cross at the interruption, but a little awed too. I often used to pray passionately that my mother would never die, my belief in prayer having been fully restored by then, for I lived in an atmosphere of simple and profound faith.

The day began with family prayers and learning a text by heart and ended with a reading from *Little Pillows* before I went to sleep. In between, there was being good or being naughty, with Jesus always at hand being pleased or sad and God listening in the background with rewards and punishments.

Next to Jesus and my mother, my brother was the most importantly loved person in my life. He was some years older than myself – there was a sister in between and another brother who had died. He was a quiet, gentle fair-haired little boy. My father thought him too shy. 'If you recite your hymn today in front of the family, Kenny, I will see about that new bicycle.' We were all at Sunday lunch (roast beef, Yorkshire pudding, two veg and apple pie). My brother got up from his seat beside me: 'Stand up, stand up for Jesus ye soldiers of the cross,' he began in a whisper, then turned crimson and rushed from the room. Consumed with a passionate sympathy I began to cry. Afterwards my mother saw to it that he got his bicycle. When he was sent away to his boarding school I could not bear it. 'My heart keeps on crying,' I said to my mother. When he came home at last for the holidays I fell downstairs and grazed my knee in my eagerness to get at him and started sobbing. He hugged me and cried a little in sympathy, big boy that he was, but he could never bear to see other people suffer and hated the sight of blood. This made my mother wonder at his early decision to become a doctor. 'But that is the reason,' he said.

I was fond of my sisters too, but not to the same degree. One day we were all four in the garden together, sitting on the lawn among the daisies, with which I was on intimate terms, and my elder sister hung a daisy chain round my neck. 'I am not ME alone,' I suddenly thought, 'I am US.'

Besides the family there was Vera, next door. She and I used to see our respective fathers off in the morning and remain afterwards swinging on our own iron gates till summoned away.

'My Daddy goes to London Town,' boasted Vera.

'Mine* goes to the City,' I replied witheringly.

The superiority of the City over London Town was obvious even to Vera. It was easy to wither her and, being the youngest

* My father was a manager of the old established Atlas Insurance Company of which he wrote a history, published by Dent and illustrated by C.E. Brock.

in my family, I enjoyed the process. I despised her because she had no conversation and was looked after by a nanny, but I also greatly envied her her little brother Rupert and her rocking-horse. I should have much liked a younger brother or sister to play with and I ardently desired a rocking-horse. I enjoyed going to tea with Vera because the nanny made a fuss of me and let me ride the rocking-horse as much as I liked, while poor Vera stood plaintively by. Sometimes I went for walks with Nanny and Vera and Rupert in his push-chair. One day the push-chair was decorated with flags. It was the end of the Boer War. My brother and sisters all wore buttons with pictures of Lord Roberts (Bobs) and Kitchener on them and waved flags. I, too, had a flag to wave and my mother said, 'Thank God that's over. We don't want any more wars ever.'

None of us children had ever had a nanny because we had a maiden aunt instead. She was my father's only sister and she loved and admired him too much to look at anyone else, which was a great pity, my mother always said. She was nice looking but very shortsighted. She wore a feather boa and sang in the Church choir and played the piano and taught me my letters and to put numbers into different homes on my slate, and to sing some songs and hymns. She also took me for walks when my mother was too busy and, on these walks, she showed me that old brick walls were beautiful. She also knew where several nice cats lived who could be stroked. She shared my love of animals, whereas my darling mother disliked them – though this did not prevent her allowing us to keep our pets.

I loved my aunt, though not as much as I loved my mother, except when I was ill, for my aunt was a born nurse.

There were two feats demanded by my aunt, however, which seemed to me excessive. First, she tried to teach me to spell by the use of cardboard letters. A word was placed before me. 'Now look at it,' my aunt said, 'until when you shut your eyes you can see it in the darkness.' This I never succeeded in doing, and it ended in me pretending that I had done so – otherwise I was afraid I would be sitting there all day. Then she expected me to sing a note at the same time as she played it.

This I thought unfair, though I was quite prepared to sing it after I had heard it.

However, I managed all the same to learn several songs. There was one about Tommy going to Sandhurst to be a soldier of the Queen, and Willie going to Osborne. There was also

> Past eight o'clock and it's bedtime for Dolly
> Past eight o'clock and it's bedtime for me
> Goodnight Mama, Goodnight Papa
> Goodnight to all the rest
> Goodnight Mama, goodnight Papa
> I must love Dolly best.

This song annoyed me because I was sent to bed long before eight and also I thought it silly and wrong to love a doll better than one's father and mother.

My mother was a busy person. She had a Bible class, ran a book club, and did temperance work, but I think she did all this from a sense of Christian duty. What she really lived for was her family and she also loved to sketch and read and write stories and poetry for children. She had some close friends and came from a large and loving family, but she did not like parties and anything in the way of formal entertainment bored and worried her. She had her At Home days every month of course, when callers came for afternoon tea and left cards, one large one for themselves and two small ones for their husbands, always two because they were not there in person. The cards were dropped unobtrusively on to a silver card-tray in the hall. It was important to look at them afterwards because the calls had to be returned. Sometimes I went with her, dressed in summer in a starched white frock and straw hat, wreathed with buttercups and fastened with elastic under my chin that was either too tight or too loose, and in winter in my coat and gaiters and muff and tippet. I also liked to attend the At Home days in my own house, when I would be allowed to

13

finish up the tiny rolls of white bread and butter after all the ladies had gone.

It was in 1902 that I went for my first motor car ride. I had never seen a car before that and I don't think I saw one again for a long while. My Uncle Laurie, who was married to my mother's sister Anne, was a black sheep, but for that day he was pure white and a hero. He was enjoying a short period of respectability and affluence, working for a motor firm, and had actually driven down in one to see us. The car pranced along our road snorting with pride and stopped at our gate. Then my uncle proceeded to give us all a ride in turn. My mother, her hat firmly tied round with a large white veil, climbed apprehensively up into the passenger seat and I squeezed in beside her. 'I'm sure I shall be sick,' said my mother. 'Nonsense, Emmie,' said my uncle. He pulled at a lever sticking out at his side and gave a resounding hoot on his horn to summon people to look at us, and off we went. Dogs began to bark, passers-by stopped and others came to their windows, the trees ran past us and the wind blew through my curls. I was amazed at this experience and it was over much too soon. We went to the end of our road and back and my mother's fears were not realized, but she decided she did not like motor cars.

She was a notoriously bad traveller by any vehicle, which was unfortunate as my father loved journeys, but could not enjoy them without her. When I was three he went to Egypt on business and took her with him. She hated leaving her home and children, especially myself, but she would not have dreamt of not accompanying him. It was an adventure then to go East. There were few, if any, tourists and it was possible to see the Pyramids and the Sphinx in solitude and to pick up curios that were lying around or to buy them very cheaply. My father brought home some little earthenware funeral lamps that were buried with the dead to light them in their journey through the Underworld. He also took a great many photographs which were proudly displayed to guests. One that was enlarged and hung in a place of honour in the dining room showed my mother sitting at each end of the Sphinx. Two snapshots had been invisibly joined together. This never failed my father as a source of interest and amusement when showing his photography.

I think they were only away for a month or so, but it seemed an age to me. My aunt, of course, was in charge, but I missed my mother badly and when this became unbearable I used to steal up to her bedroom and get inside her wardrobe to smell her clothes. On the day when my parents came home we all kept rushing to the door whenever we heard a horse and carriage along the road. At last a cab, loaded with trunks, drew up and my father and mother got out and, would you believe it, just at first they seemed like strangers and I drew back. But then, almost at once, everything was all right and the world was as it should be once more.

My first home had been a solid, comfortable, Victorian home with coloured glass panes over the front door and an uncomplicated garden of lawn, borders, and gravel paths. My second home was very different.

In those days my father was able to do what would be absolutely impossible today. On a spacious plot on a road a little further out of the town, a new house was to be built. My father was able, in advance, to rent this house (on a seven-year renewable lease) and was allowed to dictate to the architect and builder the number of rooms, the materials to be used, and the general design, as freely as if he had owned it. He was an adventurous planner and he also demanded good workmanship and good materials. These he got.* The house was built in the new fashion, influenced by Philip Webb. It was a tile-hung farmhouse, with casement windows instead of the Victorian gothic sash windows. There was to be electricity, not gas, and soon there was a telephone, which my mother always treated with distrust. She wound it up, shut her eyes tightly, gripped the ear and mouth pieces and prepared for the worst.

* The house is now divided into flats but the extremely good workmanship of the period is still evident.

The garden, created from a virgin field, had grass paths (quite an innovation and much admired), and also herbaceous borders and flowering shrubs instead of the conventional bedded-out displays of geraniums, lobelias, and calcelaria. My parents named the new home 'Oakhampstead' which is still its name today. There was a fine old oak tree dominating the garden and Hampstead was their own birthplace, as well as that of their four children.

We moved one snowy day in January 1903. My aunt and I were driven to the house in a cab piled with all sorts of odd objects. The snow was falling fast, and as soon as we arrived I was set down in front of a roaring fire in what was to be the morning room. I was tremendously excited. The room was empty except for the carpet and one little armchair in which I sat while men carried in a corner cupboard, a round table, and the piano with its fluted green silk and brass candle holders. All these belonged to my aunt, for it was to be her room. Then I was left alone. I went to look out of the window. The men were still very busy carrying in furniture and I watched the big van horses pawing and stamping in the snow. It grew dark and I began to feel lonely and bored and a little homesick for my old playroom and toys. But presently my mother came to me and I was given my supper and put to bed. I was to share the attic bedroom with my sister. The cot beside my parents' bed was a thing of the past. My excitement came back and I sang myself to sleep with a long invented rigmarole about stars and daisies. I was no longer a baby, I was a girl.

CHAPTER TWO

1903–1913
The new house, school and politics

The garden of the new home was of more importance to me than its interior. In it I experienced freedom and privacy for the first time. I was no longer afraid of being alone there as I had been in the old garden before I became a girl, though of course there were 'Presences' about that had to be reckoned with. The oak tree could always be trusted but I was not too sure about the two big elms in the field, though I was grateful to them for their offspring who made a splendid thicket in which to play. My father put up a swing for me on a branch of the oak. It was a good place for a swing, for it hung by the side of a bank with a drop to the tennis court and if you sat on it akimbo with your legs handing each side and pulled on the ropes you flew out over the world. It was like riding Pegasus. Besides the three primeval great trees that we found there, my father planted a copper beech and a weeping ash in the garden. When I visited the place more than sixty years later, most of it had been built over. The oak and the elms had vanished but my father's beech and ash had grown into noble creatures. We used to keep our croquet mallets and balls under the ash. The croquet lawn was in constant use – it was the favourite family game and we invented all sorts of exciting, unconventional ways of playing it. There were often tennis parties on summer Saturdays, with the maids bringing out strawberries and cream and lemonade. I was too young to play tennis so I watched from my swing and occasionally made myself useful retrieving balls.

But the garden was best when I had it to myself. My father had planned it with imagination and love and it was very varied, on

17

different levels divided up by lawns, banks, and winding grass paths between the herbacious borders and the fruit. There was a little hazelnut alley and a pergola, sweet with jasmine and honeysuckle and clematis, but the field was left to itself and was a mass of wild flowers in the spring and summer. It was a bird-haunted garden and the dawn chorus was deafening. There was open ground all about us and a view of the North Downs. Every morning and evening the rooks from the rookery in the trees beyond the garden would fly over the house to and fro to feeding grounds cawing like mad. There were lots of nests in the garden and I once saw a willow wren's woven among the grass in the field. I could travel from one end of the field to the other on my hands and knees tunnelling through the sorrel and moon daisies and all the different tall grasses that made green waving walls round me. I could go for miles and no-one could see me.

But my dog always knew where I was. Soon after we came to the new home I was given a puppy. He was a cross between a spaniel and a terrier, very intelligent and beautiful. I called him Pickle and he was my darling, my beloved companion. He was strictly brought up, and when he misbehaved my father sometimes beat him and I hated him for this.

Now I had half a bedroom, a dog, and the freedom of the garden. Next came another momentous happening.

I was to share a governess with three other little girls. The governess was called Miss Snow. She had hair done in a bun, and a face criss-crossed with tiny red lines, and she wore a black velvet ribbon round her neck. She took me on her lap, which I did not like because I thought I was now too old to go on people's laps except my mother's. Two of the girls, Florence and Muriel, were older than myself: Florence was pretty and gentle and not very clever; Muriel was more interesting but used to sulk. Enid who was the youngest of us four, would have been pretty too but she had a hare lip which both fascinated and repelled me. She was spoilt and when she could not have what she wanted, she would lie on the floor and scream and kick; Miss Snow could do nothing with her. This also fascinated me.

I neither liked nor disliked Miss Snow but I liked having

lessons with other children very much indeed. I was now seven years old. Every morning, as soon as Family Prayers were over, my mother would see me off to walk by myself to Florence, Muriel, and Enid's home. First I went up the garden and through a gate in our back fence and then along a footpath that skirted a big park where Jersey and Alderney cows were peacefully feeding. At the end of the footpath I had to cross a road, but there was hardly ever anything on it – perhaps a milkman's deep cart with its big brass milk cans jangled by. More dangerous was the smart little butcher's van driven at a spanking pace by the butcher's boy in a blue striped apron, but it was generally too early for him. I went by a row of small Victorian houses and a grocer's shop, crossed another road, and pressed my nose between a crack in the fence enclosing a girl's school called Laurel Bank, hoping I might see something interesting. Then came some larger houses facing a field edged with elm thicket, a good playground, and at last I reached Maycroft. The maid opened the door for me and I hung up my coat and hat and went upstairs to join Miss Snow, Florence, Muriel, and Enid at a round table covered with a red fringed tablecloth. The lesson I liked best was *Little Arthur's History of England* by Lady Callcott. At twelve o'clock we went for a walk to the common or the Park or the larch wood, where we could play while Miss Snow sat on a bench and read. On the way back I was delivered safely home. At the other side of the larch wood were some cottages, and the children who lived there sometimes came out also to play and hurled abuse at us which we in turn hurled back at them. There was no love lost between 'Board School' children and us. Later on, when I went to school, I found this feud intensified. At one time a Board School girl, older and stronger than myself, used to lie in wait for me at a certain corner and, pinning me to the wall, threatened me with her skipping rope and taunted me with being a stuck-up High School snob. I was terrified of her, though I answered back as best I could, but I never told my parents about her or about the cottage children. I knew that they would disapprove of any such

19

goings on and I myself felt guilty somehow and suppressed both my fear and my guilt.

The poor children from London, however, were in a different category. One was taught to be kind to them, and when they were sent to our town by the Children's Country Holiday Fund, I had to help entertain them. I found this embarrassing but I was truly sorry for them, living in a dreadful place called 'the slums'. London altogether was apt to frighten me when I went there with my parents to visit relations. I knew from Cruikshank's illustrations to Dickens that it contained terrible characters: old women who lay in wait to tear the clothes off one's back and villainous old men. There were also the cab horses; it was dreadful to see them whipped, and some were so thin like poor Ginger in Black Beauty and oh! the horror of seeing one lying in the road with a man sitting on his head. And there were sinister streets with straw laid on them because someone was very ill and there might be drunk men, and I saw ragged crossing sweeper boys dangerously darting between the traffic. No, London was not for me.

I do not think I learned much from Miss Snow. At length she vanished from the scene and I went to join my sister at school. It was a small Church of England High School, the only alternatives being the much larger County School for girls, recently opened, which was considered rough, or Laurel Bank, where the standard of work was low. Also my parents, though Nonconformist, preferred a place of education definitely geared to religion. There were a handful of non-Anglicans there and we were let off the Catechism lessons that preceded morning prayers, though we had to learn two or three verses of the Bible every day which we repeated to our form mistress before lessons started. I used to learn these on my way to school: 'Who, passing through the valley of Baka maketh it a well, the rain also filleth the pools,' I chanted loudly as I pushed through the gate past the church that led to an asphalt path down a hill which for ever after became that valley.

My first form mistress, Miss Croft, who taught the two lowest classes together in one room, was a stern disciplinarian. I was put to sit at the back and soon found I could not see what she was writing on the blackboard. We sat in couples on little benches with a folding desk in front of us upon which to write. I tried to see what my neighbour had copied from the board. 'You must not do that,' said Miss Croft. 'You must learn to work on your own – now Molly here is deaf and dumb, poor little girl, but she doesn't try to copy from anyone else.' I thought this very unfair because Molly could see properly, but I did not say so, nor did I tell my parents, who were quite unsuspecting as my father's short sight and my mother's long sight had worked out evenly for the other children. So my first days at school were not very happy until at last it was discovered that I needed spectacles.

This bad beginning, however, was more than compensated by my next year in Form II, where I ruled the roost. Our form mistresses taught us every subject, and during this halcyon period I was under Miss Kingsford, who was young, had a nice smile, and blushed very easily. She blushed when we coaxed her to sing to us. She sang 'Au clair de la Lune, mon ami Pierrot' in a sweet clear voice and we clapped. My best friend, Audrey, and I, who were rivals for 'top of the form', once had the cheek to invite ourselves to tea at Miss Kingsford's cottage – that is, we appeared on her doorstep at tea time. She was very kind to us and even told us to choose a present from a shelf of little china animals and other objects. Presents were few and wonderful and we were both overcome. Audrey chose a tiny china dog, but I chose a pearl-handled glove button hook. 'What a funny choice,' said Miss Kingsford, but I thought the handle was most beautiful – a pearl-handled button hook for long white kid gloves. Did Miss Kingsford go to parties wearing them? I can only see her in a stiff white blouse and tie and a belt with a silver clasp, singing 'Au clair de la lune' and blushing.

The other High School mistress whom I remember clearly was Miss Baa-Brown, who wore perfectly round steel-rimmed spectacles on a little thin beaky nose and looked just like an owl. She had a good way of teaching grammar. We underlined each part of speech with a different coloured chalk – red for verbs, green for nouns, blue for pronouns, yellow for adjectives, brown for adverbs, and a brown hook for conjunctions. It made parsing a pleasure.

The education I got at the High School was a sound basic one in English, history, geography, arithmetic and French. German or Latin was not taught till the higher two forms which I never reached. Besides grammar we learnt a great deal of poetry by heart:

> Oh Tiber, Father Tiber, to whom the Romans pray
> A Roman's arms, a Roman's life take thou in charge this
> day.

> I sprang to the stirrup, and Boris, and he,
> I galloped, Dirk galloped, we galloped all three.

> A chieftain to the Highlands bound
> Cried Boatman do not tarry.

The stirring rhythms and the rhymes were easy to memorize, splendid to declaim. I can recite many of them still. I don't remember history lessons after *Little Arthur*; I think I learnt more history from my father and from reading at home. For geography we drew maps in which most of the world was coloured pink to show it belonged to us. The British Empire was glorious and we believed it to be for the general good and everlasting. On Empire Day, we had a holiday, the only special school holiday in the year, and we went up on the Downs to pick bee and spider orchids.

The curriculum at the High School was rigidly academic, influenced still by the hard-won standards in girls' education of the last century. The higher forms sat for the junior and senior Oxford examinations. There were no crafts taught, no art except drawing of jugs, drapery, cubes, and boxes, no music, except songs from Gaudeamus. There was one period of plain sewing a week. There was optional hockey, also once a week, played on a boys' football ground at some distance from the school. I tried this for one term only but, with the long walk to and fro from home, found it too exhausting. Gym consisted of exercises and marching to a thumping piano accompaniment, which I enjoyed. I developed a special goose step of my own which I thought impressive. 'Is anything the matter with your leg, dear?' asked the mistress.

We had no plays, entertainments, or concerts, but every year we assembled in the Town Hall for Prizegiving and speeches. We wore white dresses and felt important. Everyone who scored over a certain percentage in the yearly examinations gained a prize. We did not choose our books, so they were a surprise. I received in turn *Beautiful Joe* by M. Saunders, *The Caged Lion* by Charlotte M. Yonge, and *Ivanhoe*. They were splendidly printed and bound in hard plum-coloured leather stamped in gold with the arms of the school. I was proud of them and enjoyed reading each of them very much.

I walked the two miles to school and back, first tagging behind my sister and then alone. Later, three girls from our road suddenly appeared at the beginning of one term and I was overjoyed. 'Now I shall have company,' I thought, and, besides, I had always wanted to know that family. So I waited eagerly for the end of lessons and ran up to them outside the school gate. However, Violet, the eldest, said primly, 'But we can't walk home with you until our mothers have written to ask permission.' I was amazed at such punctilious observance of the school rule that everyone else ignored, and it seemed too silly to go home on opposite sides of the road, but we did. Our mothers wrote the required notes on request and I got to know and like the two younger girls very much, but Violet I never cared for. Rosamund, the youngest, was the best friend I ever had for playing Cavaliers and Roundheads and Robin Hood.

But the friendship of my High School days, which meant much more to me than any other, was with my one-time rival. Her name was Audrey, she had untidy shoulder-length fair hair, large blue eyes set widely apart, an impudent snub nose, and one very deep dimple, and I loved her dearly. We always sat next to each other in class and, out of school, we explored the

23

countryside on our bikes, ten-year-olds, allowed to go as far as we liked and wherever we liked without fear.

We planned to produce a book, I the author, she the illustrator. She was good at drawing and had enriched my album with a painstaking copy of one of Louis Waine's comic cats. We all exchanged albums, bound in soft squishy leather, in which people who could not draw on the tinted pages copied out jokes and riddles and moral verses:

> Do the work that's nearest
> Though it's dull at whiles
> Helping when you meet them
> Lame dogs over stiles.

I began the book – a boring narrative poem about a teddy bear – but it did not get far and I don't remember Audrey producing any illustrations. We switched to ornamenting black-headed hatpins with different coloured sealing-wax. You twirled the hat pin over a little spirit lamp and applied the hot sealing wax in beautiful swirls of red and green and blue and gold. We spent all our threepence a week pocket-money on this and presented our mothers and elder sisters with the exquisite end products.

My first real sense of loss was when Audrey's family moved away to live in London. It was the end of the summer term and the last tea party I was ever to have with her. The time had come to say goodbye. She danced backwards from her gate, the sun shining through the leaves on her bouncing hair and white frock. She was waving a farewell at me, and with a horrid lump in my throat I waved back. I would not pass her house for a long time afterwards, though it was the best way to school.

We wrote regularly to one another, letters beginning 'My darling Chum', and she came to stay with me several times. I was never allowed a return visit and did not understand why. I was not told till long afterwards that Audrey's father had left the town under a cloud of unpaid debts – or so my parents believed. I do not know that I should have suffered much from that fact on a visit, but actually I preferred that Audrey should come to me. I paced up and down the platform waiting for her train, bursting with impatience. At the far end you could catch the first glimpse of the engine as it came roaring and puffing round the bend. At last I saw it rushing towards me, it drew up, and out jumped Audrey. We were to be together again for a whole week. It was my birthday. She gave me *Gems from Matthew Arnold* and *Gems from Christina Rossetti*, both bound in limp soft pink leather with flappy edges. I thought them beautiful but did not read them.

We took a picnic to a wild daffodil field that we knew. The night before at dinner, which we had with the grown-ups, she had admired our beaten coppery finger bowls set at the side of each plate. 'What kind do you have?' I enquired casually. 'Oh, china,' she said, but later that night she whispered, 'There's something I want to say to you tomorrow.' It sounded as though it was very important and interesting. Among the daffodils she said miserably, 'Now I must tell you what I said I would – I told a lie about those finger bowls, we haven't got any.' I was disappointed – it wasn't at all interesting after all. 'Oh never mind,' I said quickly. 'Let's have our picnic now.'

Our friendship flourished until we were both about fourteen – then we suddenly stopped writing to each other. After I had left school and was working at home for Oxford, we made one attempt to renew the relationship. Our skirts were hobbled and our hair was up and she was engaged to a young officer called Bob, and our meeting was not a success. We both recognized that we had drifted apart too much for any renewal and I never saw her again, but she was my first taste of the enormous joy in friendship that has enriched my whole life.

One day when I was just turned thirteen I came home from school feeling ill. My mother took my temperature and put me to bed in the spare room, which was always a sign of serious trouble. I felt hotter and hotter and ached all over. In the morning the doctor came and proclaimed that I had rheumatic fever. I never went back to the High School again, so I never properly left or said goodbye to anyone. This did not worry me much – I was feeling too ill.

I had been ill a number of springs before – bronchitis, whooping cough, a threatened mastoid, and tonsils and adenoids which were removed in my mother's bedroom. I lay on a trestle table, the sickly sweet chloroform stifling me from a mask clamped over my face. When I came to, I was back in bed and my mother made me a cowslip ball to take away the smell of the chloroform. Our family doctor was very kind and attentive. At our first home the doctor used to pay his calls with his horse and carriage.

I can only remember a very few medicines, fig syrup and odious, odious cod liver oil, a pink cough mixture, a few drops of eucalyptus on a lump of sugar, and camphorated oil to rub on one's chest. My aunt's firm hand went round and round and the smell was quite pleasant and then a piece of flannel was applied. There were bread poultices too, back and front, as hot as you could stand them, and a bronchitis kettle with a long spout on the coal fire that was kept briskly going, night and day. For a cold you sat with your feet and legs in a pail of mustard and water.

After these illnesses my mother took me to Brighton to convalesce where my grandfather and little deaf aunt lived. We had rooms in a tall, bow-fronted house whose large windows looked out over the sea and the narrow side ones gave an interesting view of streets with their ceaseless pageant of horses and carriages, donkeys, goat carts, bicycles, and people of all sorts. Brighton was full of glory. There was the little railway along the front that at high tide actually rode the breaking waves. It went all the way to Black Rock at the foot of the bold empty Downs and at the terminus there was an old man with a 'Happy Family': a dog, a cat, a monkey, a rabbit, and a canary, all on good terms with each other. You dropped pennies in a box for the privilege of seeing them. Then there was the pier which stretched out further and further and further from the shore with its end crustated with ancient perpetual fishermen. At intervals it had magic machines that a penny would set going. You could shoot a football goal or set a horse galloping to the winning post or send a silver ball into the centre of a maze if you had a penny to spare. Inland a little way was the Pavilion, desolate, delapidated, and deserted. 'A monstrosity,' said my father, who agreed with Queen Victoria. I thought it mysterious and sad.

It was at Brighton that my mother and I saw our first aeroplane. It was the year that Blériot made the first air channel crossing. All along the front there was a waiting, excited crowd. Then at last it came, a strange great clumsy ugly creature low down, only just above the line of the breaking waves. It was like something out of a comic fairy tale. 'Horrible,' said my mother dismissively.

After rheumatic fever, my father took my mother and me to the Malvern hills and I was pushed about in a bath-chair which was sometimes terrifying for my father used to rush me down hills and I was afraid of being tipped out. I graduated from a bath-chair to a little pony trap with a lazy pony called Tommy. I was allowed to drive him along the quiet empty lanes and my father taught me about church architecture in the Worcestershire villages. When the first nasty days of the rheumatic fever were over I did not mind being ill at all. I could read as much as I liked without people chasing me out to *do* things, for whether I was well or ill I lived more than half my life in the world of books.

We were a reading family. There were books in every room of the house and I was given the free run of them. My parents would not have thought it possible that I should find anything harmful on their shelves. Once, though, my father discovered Oscar Wilde's *Importance of Being Ernest* among my brother's books. He burnt it. *The Channings* by Mrs Henry Wood had also unaccountably appeared one day and was frowned upon. I had to finish it in bed under the clothes – a double sin. I was not supposed to read in bed as it was bad for the sight. Nor was I supposed to read in the mornings unless I was unwell, a prohibition which has stayed with me all my life to a certain degree. I had hide-outs, therefore, crouching behind the sofa in the sitting room or among the bushes in the field. My reading ranged with equal avidity at this period from *Chatterbox* to

27

Dickens, and to Carlyle's *French Revolution* which made a great impression. I did not need always to understand what I read. There was something beyond understanding – 'Robespierre, sea green and incorruptible' – such phrases filled me with an excited satisfaction.

The late nineteenth century to the first World War was a vintage period for children's books. This was when the great classics were appearing – the Alice books, Lear's Nonsense rhymes, *Westward Ho, the Water Babies, Treasure Island, Little Women, Black Beauty, Huckleberry Finn,* the *Just So* stories, *Puck of Pook's Hill*, George Macdonald's Curdie Books, *The Wind in the Willows, The Secret Garden*, and the works of Beatrix Potter and E. Nesbitt. Most of these were being published in my childhood and provided blessed birthday and Christmas presents.

My father read aloud well and enjoyed doing it. Most winter evenings he would read to the family, gathered together round a roaring fire in the sitting-room. My mother would have her knitting, and we children would settle down to any occupation that left our ears free. More often than not he read Scott or Dickens. Thackeray was disapproved of for his cynicism, Hardy of course was unacceptable, and somehow Trollope does not seem to have been known much then. Sometimes my father would read poetry – Tennyson, Browning's narrative poems, Longfellow, and bits of *Paradise Lost* and Shakespeare. King Henry's speech at Agincourt was a favourite. My mother also read aloud to me, especially when I was ill. She liked books about ordinary, nice people best. She did not really care for anything fantastic or too romantic or melancholy. She was always on the side of 'sanity and humour'. 'In sooth I know not why I am so sad,' she would quote mockingly when gloom was around. I benefited by the books she bought secondhand from Mudie's for her book club:* contemporary novels by George Macdonald, Conan Doyle, Elizabeth,† E.F. Benson, G.K.

* This book club was organized and run by my mother for members of the church.
† *Elizabeth and the German Garden* etc:

28

Chesterton, and many a good second-class novelist, altogether forgotten now.

We took in a number of papers – there were so many available then. *The Times* regularly and also, but not I think every day, the *Manchester Guardian* (now the *Guardian*) and the *Chronicle*. This was because a cousin was on the staff of the *Manchester Guardian* under its famous founder C.P. Scott and another cousin, A.J. Cummings, was sub-editor of the *Chronicle*. We also took the green *Westminster Gazette, Punch*, the *Illustrated London News, The British Weekly* (a nonconformist paper), *The Bookman*, and the *Spectator* (no Sunday papers, of course). I wallowed in all of these, especially *Punch* and the *Illustrated London News*, cutting out its pictures to paste into my very dull diary. But my especial delight was the monthly *Little Folds* with its thrilling serials – oh, the agony of having to wait another four weeks to know what happened in 'The Scarlet Pikesman'! Bella Sydney Woolf (sister-in-law to Virginia) was a sub-editor and ran a letter and competition page to which I contributed and sometimes won prizes.

Little Folks was for some reason later supplanted by Arthur Mee's *Children's Encyclopaedia* and *Children's Newspaper* which were less enjoyable. Occasionally there was a bonus in the way of *The Strand Magazine*, then serializing both E. Nesbit's magical stories and *Sherlock Holmes*. I don't know why we didn't take in this marvellous magazine regularly, but it only seemed to appear when my brother was at home.

All these papers were well printed, without printers' errors, on good paper, containing few advertisements and relatively few pictures. They taught me much about the life going on around me. So did listening to grown-ups' conversation at mealtimes, when I was not expected to talk much myself. My father was a Gladstonian Liberal, and both he and my mother took a keen interest in politics, though church matters always came first. Queen Victoria, Prince Albert, and Mr Gladstone shone in an aura of heroic grace for my father, and Edward VII, Mr Asquith, and Mr Lloyd George could not hope to compete. The King's infidelity, his love of horse-racing, and his general easy attitude to life were all matters for grave regret. Luckily, the private lives of Asquith and Lloyd George were not yet public property and both were accounted worthy of respect though not of hero-worship. Mr Lloyd George, especially, was highly commended for his inauguration of old age pensions and health insurance.

My first clear political memories are of the great Liberal victory of 1906. The voting went on for a week. We all wore rosettes – blue and white for Liberals in those days, yellow and purple for the Tories. My Board School terror pounced on me at her dreaded corner, tore off my blue rosette, and threw it in the gutter. She was flaunting the yellow and purple. I pinned on another rosette and went about singing 'Stamp, stamp, stamp upon Protection' and grew more and more excited until the day when the poll was to be declared. We drove in a carriage decorated with blue ribbons to swell the crowd before the Municipal Buildings, where there was then a large open space and fields. The two candidates were Mr Brodie for the Liberals and Mr Rawson for the Conservatives. Even today the name Rawson carries with it a sinister shadow, whereas Brodie faintly shines with virtue and charm. (I have never actually met a Brodie or a Rawson in the flesh.) After what seemed a very long time of suspense, the Mayor, the candidates, and some other gentlemen, including my father, came out onto the balcony and Mr Brodie was declared the winner. But at the next election in 1910 I wrote in my diary: 'There has been a General Election this week and the Conservative, Mr Rawson, has been returned by a shameful majority, but thank goodness, the Liberals are in power in the government.' My best friend Audrey said to me, 'It *is* a pity you're a Liberal and I'm a Conservative, but we're both Oxford and that's what *really* matters.'

On May 6th 1910 I wrote in my diary, 'Late last night at 11.45 His Majesty King Edward VII went away to Heaven at *His* King's command. All Great Britain and many foreign countries are mourning him. Queen Alexandra is now called the Queen Mother.' There follows an affecting picture cut from the *Illustrated London News* of the Queen placing a white rose in the hands of the dead King. I outlined this picture with ivory black from my paintbox. We went to see the funeral procession. It was a very hot day and we had seats on a stand in Cambridge Terrace, but alas the crowd was so thick that we could not get to them. I was always frightened of crowds and what with that and the heat and the disappointment I burst into tears. Immediately the crowd, impassable and obdurate before, made way for us. Triumphant and duly grateful to me my family proceeded to their seats.

'The Kings of Spain, Portugal, Italy, Greece, Norway and Denmark, Belgium, and the Emperors of Germany and Austria attended the funeral', I wrote, 'and many Queens and other famous men. We had a very good view of Lord Roberts, Kitchener, the Emperor of Germany, the Prince and the little Princess Mary who is just exactly a year older than I – also of the poor Queen Mother, the King's horse and favourite dog Ces-"' (the spelling of Caesar defeated me). I was, I remember especially, struck by the Kaiser, sitting very upright with a shining helmet on a white horse, and thought him far more impressive than King George. A year later, in July, I rather casually noted in my diary, 'A good many things have happened lately, for instance the coronation.'

My mother was involved with the women's suffrage movement, though she was emphatic that she was a suffra*gist* not a suffra*gette*. She strongly disapproved of breaking windows, slashing pictures, and assaulting policemen and politicians, and shook her head sadly over imprisonments, forcible feeding, and the tragedy of Emily Davidson and the King's horse at the Derby. She used to argue against these extremes with one of her friends and thought it rather silly when this same friend gave a party with a huge cake iced in green, purple, and white, the suffragette colours. But she brought me home a piece of the cake.

More important to her was the cause of temperance. The Band of Hope was for 'the working classes' but my mother canvassed enthusiastically on behalf of the middle class Young Abstainers' Union. The pledge not to touch alcohol, however, was the same for both. All the children of our church seemed to belong to the Y.A.U. and we had very enjoyable parties at each other's houses, not much incommoded by a speaker who would tell us about the Temperance Hospital (to which we sent boxes of primroses in the spring) and emphasize the evils of drink. These were very vivid to me and I looked upon public houses, and even country inns, as dens of iniquity. The idea that I should ever enter one was unthinkable. None of the families with which we were intimate ever dreamed of having any alcoholic drink in their houses, though at Christmas time we did have blue flames round our Christmas pudding. How did those blue flames come to be there?

Besides the Liberals and the suffragists and the Young Abstainers, there were missionaries. Support for them was important and obligatory. On the rare occasions when we were given money, a portion of it always had to go into the missionary box on the playroom mantlepiece. Missionaries home from abroad on leave were sometimes our honoured guests. Missionary bazaars and magic lantern meetings were frequent and well attended. I enjoyed both, but especially the latter. You sat in the Church Hall in the dark in front of a white stretched sheet with a smelly oil lamp somewhere behind and suddenly and quite magically you saw on the screen in front of you an elephant, or an impossible temple, or palm trees and deserts. 'In Greenland's icy mountains to India's coral strand' the poor heathen were waiting to be rescued from their idols. My brother and I were both secretly very afraid that we ought to become missionaries. 'For my sake and the gospels' go and tell Salvation's story'; that hymn sounded like a knell on our hearts.

CHAPTER THREE

1903–1913
The lighter side of life

There were of course social gatherings other than Y.A.U. meetings and missionary magic lantern shows. There were Christmas parties in the winter and hay parties in the summer. 'Hurry up, the cab's at the door!' I clutched my string bag to me and hurried. I was wearing a green cloak and hood (which I wished had been red because of Little Red Ridinghood) with underneath my party frock of shantung silk or a thin cashmere or nun's veiling. We all wore white or pale colours to parties. My sleeves were short and I had white silk mittens, brown wollen stockings, and button boots which would be changed into flat-soled bronze slippers fastened with crossed elastic.

At our parties we played games – Musical Chairs, Oranges and Lemons that ended in a tug of war, General Post, Hunt the Slipper, French and English, Blind Man's Buff. Sometimes, delightfully, there were charades; Dumb crambo was not exciting but proper charades, acting a word and dressing up, was my favourite of all party pleasures. There was a sit-down feast of jellies and cake, and always crackers, but never presents. Nor can I remember any birthday parties. One kept one's birthday privately with the family and did not expect or get presents or cards from outside. The parties generally began at four o'clock and ended at seven.

A little, but only a little, later and more sophisticated were the parties that said 'Dancing'. Then the carpet was rolled back and tiny dance-cards and pencils were provided which you hoped would soon be filled up. Someone would begin to thump out dance tunes on the piano and we would whirl away

33

in polkas or waltzes. Often included was 'The Lancers', a surviving square dance (not a revival), and we invariably ended with Sir Roger de Coverley.

In the summer, when the horses and the mower had finished in the fields, we had hay parties there – tossing about the newly-mown grass swathes, burying each other, and, incidentally, helping to dry it. Here there was infinite space for play and infinite supplies of cherries and strawberries and cream. Sometimes the parties ended with rides on the top of the haywain, with the horses pulling us and the hay at a leisurely pace across the fields. For hay parties I would wear a holland smock or a pink, blue, or white starched cotton frock but never, oh never, my heart's desire – a sailor suit, navy and white, with a whistle in the side pocket and a round sailor's cap with H.M.S. Victory or Britannia on the ribbon in gold. My mother thought this costume affected and silly.

Parties were always family affairs, held in friends' own homes and gardens and fields. Entertaining at restaurants or hotels was unheard of. Treats, such as a visit to the Zoo or the Tower of London, were rare. My parents did not approve of circuses or pantomimes and my father had a life-long moral distrust of the professional theatre. I was taken once, unforgettably, to *Peter Pan* with Pauline Chase as Peter, and to an amateur local production of *The Gondoliers*, but otherwise I did not enter a theatre till I was eighteen when my brother, home from the Front, took me to my first musical. 'And did you once see Shelley plain?' Alas not! Nor, as I might have done, Sarah Bernhardt and Irvine, or Ellen Terry at her best (but I did see her in the 1920s on her seventieth birthday at the Old Vic as Portia, and it was as if I had never read or heard the famous 'Mercy' speech before). As for cinemas – they were one worse than theatres, and again I was turned eighteen and staying away with friends when I saw my first film – Mary Pickford in *Rebecca at Sunnybrook Farm*. But I did not feel seriously deprived for no-one in my circle frequented theatres or cinemas. Florence, Muriel, Enid, and my best friend,

Audrey, were taken to the Pantomime or to *Where the Rainbow Ends* at Christmas and that's about all.

Besides I was not starved of drama. Far from it. The curtain rises on *Scenes from David Copperfield* and my piping voice opens the proceedings: 'Peggotty, were you ever married? You're a very handsome woman you know.' The 'handsome woman' was one of my elder sister's friends. She had round red cheeks, dark eyes, became a missionary in Formosa, and lived to be a hundred. My brother performed, and well performed, the somewhat amazing feat of doubling the parts of Uriah Heep and Ham Peggotty, my sister was Miss Murdstone, and I, to my enormous profit and delight, was cast as little David until he had to become too miserable-looking and thin for my plump self. A pale boy called Cecil took over. I comforted myself by knowing I could do it better and that after all he had only one scene to my three. I ignored Cecil but made friends with 'Little Emily' who was invested, for me, with a mournful and romantic interest because she was an orphan dressed in deep black except for her white pinafore and had a baby sister called Joy who was mysteriously born after her father had died. I did not know such a thing could be. I knew her part as Little Emily better than she did, in fact I knew everybody's part, and ate and drank and slept David Copperfield for weeks.

The year after, the same amateur group performed *Scenes from A Mill on the Floss* but, alas! another little girl, somebody's sister, had to have her turn and was Maggie Tulliver and I wasn't pretty or fair or sweet enough for Lucy. I ardently hoped that some catastrophe would befall the other child, but she was strong and healthy. However, I was allowed to attend all the rehearsals and lived with Maggie and Tom and the aunts and uncles as I had done with Peggotty and Miss Trotwood and the others. The impact of these two productions was tremendous, possibly all the stronger because I had never been to a theatre or a film. For the first time, though not perhaps consciously, I felt part of a wider world, involved in a serious 'grown up' enterprise, and absorbed by two great works of genius. The curious thing is that, though the tone of voice and appearance of each of those long-ago actors and actresses are as clear as daylight to me still, I have no recollection of why, or where, or to whom we performed, nor how it was received. I suspect that there was a collecting box somewhere for temperance or missionaries, but emphatically 'the play was the thing'.

We were not really a musical family but live music of a sort had a place in almost every middle-class home. My elder sister played the violin quite well and my second sister accompanied her on the piano, and they were expected to play to my father and visitors in the evenings. The strains of their performances penetrated to my bedroom and mingled with my dreams. I too, in my turn, learnt my piano pieces to play to company.

My mother was quite unmusical, but my father enjoyed music in a limited, entirely emotional way, especially favouring Handel, Mendelssohn, and the earlier Beethoven. My aunt used to sing the contralto solos from the Messiah, and the church choir made us all familiar with Parry and Stamford. We attended occasional local concerts but for the most part how silent was the air about me! When music sounded, however, it was attended to.

My wider musical experience came with the purchase of our first gramophone which had a picture of 'His Master's Voice' on it and a large horn. When my cousin, Bruce Cummings (W.N.P. Barbellion, the diarist) came to stay with us for a time, he bought a record of Wagner's *Tannhauser* and put it on from morning till night. 'Oh Bruce!' said my mother, '*do* stop that, it's like a lot of cats on the roof.'

But this gramophone was not my earliest experience of such marvels. Earlier, round about 1908, another cousin, a boy of my own age, had come for a visit and brought with him a little phonograph. Its records were wax cylinders which you slipped onto a drum and then you wound it up. This magic machine completely threw the old tinkling musical box into the shade. There were three records – Harry Lauder (the funniest songs on earth), 'Take a pair of sparkling eyes' (the most romantic of all possible melodies), and 'The Soldiers' chorus" from *Faust* (the most rousing). These we played over and over again and they didn't seem to worry my mother like Wagner.

I don't know how my cousin came to be possessed of such a marvel, as his family had no money to spare. My own particular treasures, apart from books, were few and mostly second-hand or home-made – a fine, large Noah's Ark that had belonged to my father when a little boy, but whose animals now were mostly lacking paint or a leg; a beautifully-clothed doll, dressed by my sister and passed down from her together with a well-worn cradle and pram; and a doll's house made of orange boxes. But the china face of my doll and the furniture of the doll's house were finely fashioned by craftsmen.

My father (in common with many) often gave presents that he liked himself and thought we ought to like. He once gave me a picture of a little girl saying her prayers and surrounded by her dolls, similarly engaged. I had to pretend I liked this picture which shared a place of honour on the walls of our nursery (or play-room) with Landseer's 'Dignity and Impudence', 'When did you last see your Father?', and an illuminated verse of Charles Kingsley's:

Be good sweet maid and let who will be clever,
Do noble things, not dream them all day long,
And so make Life, Death and that vast Forever
One grand sweet Song.

When teddy bears first crossed the Atlantic, my father gave me a small, white one because he thought it unusual. Personally, I decided that was why my poor bear looked at me so sadly from his deep-set little black eyes, and I tried to forget he was not the right colour.

Treats, like toys, were well savoured. An early one was riding with my mother on the top of the horse-drawn omnibus from one end of the town to the other. We would alight at the terminus for a bun and a glass of milk at Mrs Cook's cake shop. She really was called, appropriately, Mrs Cook, just as inappropriately, our little dressmaker was called Miss Worsefold. My mother was the chief source of my treats. She had the lovely quality of unexpectedness. 'It's too fine a day for school,' she might suddenly say. 'Let's go to Brighton instead and see Grandpa.' And off we would go, gloriously. But actually it was always a treat just to have my mother to myself, on a bus, by the sea, among her flowers, or by the sitting room fire in winter with the maid bringing in dripping toast.

The big annual treat, our summer holiday, however, was planned and carried out by my father, a fact that should be remembered with gratitude for they were wonderful. But, truth to say, to have him let loose on us day in day out for a whole month was a strain, especially in the company of my elder sister. They both had the same flaring tempers and there were sometimes terrifying rows. My brother pointed out to me, long after, that this was the reason why our holidays were often shared by an aunt or a cousin or a friend – to keep the atmosphere temperate.

We made up quite a large company, filling two cabs bound for the station, piled with trunks and bags and bicycles. Crossing London was never pleasurable: the cab horse might look thin and miserable and might be whipped, and perhaps there might be a throng of carts and cabs and omnibuses and carriages at crossings which the policemen would take a long while to sort out and we should miss our train at King's Cross or Paddington.

Once we had arrived at the main station, though, all was pleasant. There was a second-class carriage reserved for us, and wicker lunch baskets, and we settled down comfortably. My brother noted down the name of our engine and bestowed on it his blessing. We thought of it as a live tame dragon, snorting and puffing and breathing out smoke and sparks of fire, which would presently move majestically off on its long journey. There were many joys in travelling in a corridor train. You could run up and down seeing who was in the different carriages or stand with your nose pressed against the big clean

window, spellbound. Of course I knew my Robert Louis
Stevenson *Garden of Verses*:

> Faster than fairies, faster than witches,
> Bridges and houses, hedges and ditches ...
>
> Here is a cart run away in the road
> Lumping along with man and load
> And here is a mill and there is a river
> Each a glimpse and gone forever.'

I was just turned eight and we were going to Scotland to the
Isle of Arran. The journey ended in a paddle steamer and a
sleepy drive from Brodick to the Manse at Glen Sannox. The
Minister and his wife had turned out of the Manse for the
summer and were living in a nearby cottage. She milked the
cow, Daisy, for our breakfast every morning and he preached
to us and a handful of crofters in the little kirk joined on to the
Manse, which we entered by a door from the sitting-room. The
money from letting the Manse helped to pay the university fees
for their daughter, Jean, in Glasgow.

I was at first charmed with my little box bed in the wall, until
I saw an earwig on the pillow. Earwigs, so Laurie our
housemaid had assured me, crept into your ears, had families
inside your head, and sent you mad. I called for help and the
earwig was removed but the next night there was another
waiting for me. 'There must be a nest somewhere,' said my
mother. I refused to get into the bed, but my brother came to
the rescue. 'She can change bedrooms with me,' he said. 'I
don't mind earwigs.' Somehow I knew that earwigs wouldn't
dare to harm my brother and I loved him for letting me have
his bed.

I loved him very much again one day when the family set off
to climb Goat Fell. 'I'm afraid it's too tiring an expedition for
you,' they said. 'You won't mind playing by yourself this
morning, will you? Mrs Macpherson will give you your
dinner.' But my brother said, 'Not if I carry her pig-a-back up

the mountain.' So he did and we went ahead and got to the top before all the others, and we lay on the heather waiting for them, very pleased with ourselves. But on some other occasions I was left behind, and it was on one of these that I remember being, for the first time, conscious of beauty. I had crossed the burn that ran through the neighbouring glen and I stood still among the heather beside the brown clear water, with the laden rowan trees bending over it and the glen stretching out to meet the mountain slopes, and I knew that it was beautiful.

The next year, however, I had company of my own age and do not ever remember being alone. The boy cousin, he who owned the phonograph, was invited to come to Cornwall with us, to a farmhouse where the farmer owned two beautiful chestnut horses called Polly and Bess. When he had time he would drive us in his wagonette to the almost solitary beaches of Kymance Cove or to Land's End. We took it in turns to sit high up beside him, where we had a splendid view of the harvest fields with their sprinkling of scarlet poppies and blue cornflowers and where I was sometimes allowed to hold the reins. I admired everything about Polly and Bess, including the fascinating way they managed to do their big jobs, without slowing down in the least, lifting up their lovely tails neatly and never soiling their harness.

The beaches were so empty that I was allowed to bathe in a pair of bathing drawers instead of the dress of navy serge trimmed with white braid, with trousers coming halfway down the legs and a little skirt that buttoned round the waist, that my sisters had to wear. This was daring of my mother, and she was dubious but indulgent. At the end of that holdiay my cousin and I were so sure that we would come back to that celestial place the very next summer that we buried our toy boat which had sailed the streams and pools on many a voyage with us. We buried it to await us, digging its hiding place well above the high water mark. I hope some other child found it for we neither of us ever saw that lovely shore again.

When I was twelve we had my first holiday abroad, in Paris

and then Switzerland. For the first time I heard, incredulously, children talking to each other *in French* and saw grown-up men (sailors) embracing each other. Later, in my first hotel, I could not sleep for the iron wheels and the horses' hooves clattering on the French cobbles. We went sightseeing – I was enchanted by the Winged Victory in the huge Louvre and paid my respects to the Venus of Milo, though privately I did not think much of her – she was too static and solid.

The journey to Switzerland ended on mules. I could not believe my luck – all the family (plus an aunt) climbing up and up a mountain path, strung out in a long line of clever, lovely mules. There was a carpet of autumn crocus round the little hotel and a vast view of snow-covered mountains that turned pink every evening. There were two children called Mark and Gabrielle who belonged to the place, with whom I played. I knew only a few words of French and they a mysterious half-sentence in English – 'not a very good opinion of the black' – which they repeated with pride, but we got on together very well.

On this holiday, I filled pages of my diary with florid descriptions: 'The scenery was mountains covered with pine forests, here and there a green green patch dotted with chalets and bare bleak tops – in the distance the pure, pure snow mountains pointing up to heaven, here and there a glittering waterfall and the blue blue sky over all.' The fete held in honour of 'the *supposed* birthday of the Virgin Mary' takes three pages.

It was the first time I had come in contact with Roman Catholicism, horrifying in England because of bloody Queen Mary and poor Rose being burnt in Westward Ho, and deeply disapproved of by my parents, but somehow all right abroad. But the superiority of England and the English in everything but mountains was unquestioned by everyone including (to our faces at least) the foreigners themselves. When we arrived back at Charing Cross my mother said, 'Now for a decent cup of tea at last, and how nice to be able to leave our luggage on the platform while we have it and to know it will be quite safe.'

For an English child of the middle classes living in a country town, life seemed incredibly secure. Nothing much changed; the fields and woods around me remained unthreatened. I never thought the landscape *could* alter. The shops I had known all my life were the same from year to year and prices did not alter either. Families sometimes moved away and others came, but not often and they always remained intact. I had never heard of divorce or broken homes. War was something that now belonged to history. The Kaiser sometimes forgot himself and behaved stupidly, so my father said, but after all he was Queen Victoria's grandson. So was the Tzar, who had all those pretty daughters and the little Tzarovitch, whose pictures I cut out of the *Illustrated London News* to paste into my diary. Our splendid Navy kept the peace all over the world, or at least all over the parts that mattered. At home, as was right and proper, the Liberals were still in power and were making things better for 'the poor'. As for disease and death, I was lucky enough not to come very close to them as a child, in which I was more fortunate than Victorian children and also perhaps than children today who constantly see and hear tragedy broadcast. My nearest encounter was when I was taken to see a great friend of my mother's who was very ill with tuberculosis and having open air treatment in a little hut in the garden. I also heard of other TB cases, but never of cancer. 'Bomb' was another word I never heard.

Yes, it was all very safe in my happy comfortable home except for the knowledge of Heaven and Hell and the terrible Judgement Day when the sheep would be separated from the goats. For, as I grew near my teens, I became more and more afraid that I was a goat.

CHAPTER FOUR

1903–1913
Family prayers and family servants

My father had experienced a spiritual conversion alone on the beach at Hastings when he was nineteen years old. I was always thankful, though it was a source of regret and anxiety to her, that my mother had had no such conversion, for my father's deep love and respect for her forced him to the conclusion that a sudden and immediate encounter with God was not absolutely necessary for salvation. He was anxious enough about his children as it was, believing that it was his duty to present us faultless, or as near faultless as possible, before the Lord. But besides being a duty, his religion was also his hobby and permeated his life and, because he was the sort of man who had to impose his enthusiasms and convictions on others, especially on his children, it also permeated *our* lives and often oppressed us.

The day began with Family Prayers directly after breakfast. Not that this was unusual then; in our circle it was an accepted custom, but when I went on a visit I found that in *that* household, Family Prayers were shorter and more formal and to miss them was accounted discourteous but not sinful. Our Prayers were embarrassingly personal, including, as they sometimes did, family problems, troubles, and joys, for my father's prayers were always extempore and they and the Bible readings were of arbitrary length and sometimes made me agonizingly late for school. It was my job to ring the bell three times for the maids to file in. As soon as he heard this summons, my dog would get up and stalk out of the room; the cat remained behind, looking on.

The first poem I had published in an adult magazine was called 'Family Prayers':

How still the room has grown.
The quiet bent bodies wait alone
For their spirits which have fled
And with bright eyes, prayer – proof,
Only the cat remains aloof,
Watching the jug, white, like milk.
Even the father, who speaks
Now loud, now low, as he seeks
To praise or plead; he too goes
Wandering among bright ghosts,
Sins, sorrows, saints, the hosts
That trample the painted skies.

The kneeling child sees nought
But the pictures faintly wrought
Round the old needlework box.
All day she is too tall
And she forgets, until prayers call.
And then she opens her eyes
And looking down
She sees a little blue town
All made out of blue sky
And a blue dancing girl
Kisses her hand to a swirl
Of little gold leaves, brighter far
Than old beeches. Then a sea
Like a pearl-handled knife
And a red-cloaked fisherman's wife –And the pearl sea
    sings like a shell.
The last 'Amen' sounds plain
Quickly the room fills again
And the cat
Waves his tail, and welcomes them back.

For my father, Family Prayers were the pivot of our life together. When he was driving with me to my wedding he begged me earnestly to make it the pivot of mine. I was evasive. Over the years I had become skilled in evasion though on occasions, especially when I felt my mother was on my side, I rebelled. Surprisingly, perhaps, we did not have Family Prayers again in the evenings, but for some time I had to say my nightly prayers aloud to my father and he was not content with any words but my own – I had to make them up. I did not object to making up my own prayers – it was having to do this aloud and when my father was listening that I hated. Eventually my mother sensed that this was so and intervened.

Sundays were field days for my father. They were, then, entirely different from weekdays. Of course there were no shops open and no places of entertainment; people stayed at home, wore their best clothes, and went to church. Our church was Presbyterian and the minister was a Scot. I always knew then, and forever after, that God has a Scotch accent. My father was an Elder and carried out various regular church duties. He stood in the porch with his beautifully-brushed top hat and a buttonhole in a little silver holder welcoming the congregation, and he often took up the collection and read a lesson. He read much better than anyone else, doing full justice to the lovely miracle of the Authorized Version.

When he was ninety my father read a lesson on BBC radio. I was on holiday in the Lakes at the time and, as I listened, I was looking out of our cottage at the mountains, rugged against the evening light. The voice of 'the old war horse' (as he was then affectionately known among his friends) had lost none of its resonance. It rang out triumphantly over the air, telling the story of Shadrach, Meshach, and Abednego in the burning fiery furnace. 'If it be so our God whom we serve is able to deliver us, But *if not*, be it known unto thee, O King, that we will *not* serve thy gods, nor worship the golden image which thou has set up.' I was moved and proud of him then, and I think I was a little proud listening to him as a child, sitting swinging my legs in our pew in church – but I was

45

always very glad when the service was over. It was long, especially the sermon, which averaged about forty minutes. Presbyterian ministers were noted for their scholarly dissertations. Some children were allowed to go out before the sermon and some had books or drawing materials to amuse them. I both envied and despised them as I passed the time counting the score of bald heads and blue bonnets, and playing with my gloves or my fingers until reproved by a disapproving look from my mother.

We knew just about everyone in the congregation and, as we were generally among the first arrivals, I could watch all the other families filing in. There were the Duncans, five girls and a boy to end up with, the Bells, one girl at the head and five boys following, the Macdonalds, three girls and three boys. The huge Victorian families had disappeared but those I knew averaged from five to seven or eight. Besides the long sermon there was always a children's address and special hymn, two Bible readings, and substantial extempore prayers, so that when at last I got home again I was hungry for my Sunday dinner. I wonder now when, where, and how our maids got to a church service, for I can't believe my parents' care for their spiritual welfare stopped with their required attendance at Family Prayers. Yet I don't remember anything but a rather more ample midday meal than usual on Sundays.

In the afternoon I had to go to a Children's Service which took the place of Sunday School. It was a boring affair conducted by two elderly members of the congregation in turn, though I quite enjoyed the hymns and larking about with the other children before and afterwards. The walk to and fro between fields and a row of plump chestnut trees I shared with the girl who took the part of Maggie Tulliver instead of me in *Scenes from the Mill on the Floss*. We were supposed to be friends because our elder sisters were, but we never liked each other much. However, we were drawn together on Sunday afternoons by our mutual boredom. This, for a time, was much mitigated by stealing afterwards into the church from the hall where the service had taken place and playing at 'ministers and congregation'. We took it in turns, sacrilegiously, to climb up into the pulpit itself and preach. But after a few Sundays we were discovered and complaints were made to our parents, who, alas, were dreadfully grieved and reproachful.

I was not expected to go to church a third time until I was older, and was left at home to amuse myself, but in strictly Sunday ways, for ordinary weekday pursuits were taboo and I had Sunday toys and Sunday books. I was allowed to play with the Noah's Ark (because of its Biblical connection) and I had a special Sunday doll. This doll had been bought and dressed by my grandmother for her granddaughters to play with when they visited her, and when she died it was given to me. She had a singularly sweet expression on her finely-moulded little china face. Her clothes were beautifully stitched and embroidered – she had a little bodice, padded stays, long white knickers, a flannel petticoat, a white petticoat, and a dark red cashmere dress. She also possessed a pink feather-stitched flannel nightdress and a little white nightcap. I called her Annie after my grandmother, but she was too holy to play with except on Sunday. All the week she lived in a drawer in my mother's room and I revered rather than loved her. I was also allowed to use my paintbox to illuminate texts which I chose for myself and printed carefully on postcards.

For Sunday reading, I had Bunyan's *Pilgrim's Progress* and a number of children's books that had been dear to my parents: *Ministering Children, The Golden Staircase, Stepping Heavenwards, The Wide, Wide World*; their titles tell their own stories. I found them depressing, for the children in them were unnaturally good and, even though they ofted died young, never failed to impress everyone with their courage and piety. Before I went to bed there was often another short Bible reading and an evening hymn, and at last the long day was over.

Sundays had an atmosphere of their own; they smelt of starched clothes, of polished pine pews, of the sprigs of Southernwood that my aunt sometimes gave me to take to the

service, and they resounded to church bells and to hymn tunes
and to our minister's voice going on and on. I felt them
oppressive. Their demands and their prohibitions interfered
with ordinary, cheerful life. How relieved I was on Good
Friday when we came back from the service to see my mother
pick up a gardening tool. 'It isn't like Sunday after all,' I
thought, for she would never have done such a thing on a
Sunday.

But I did not question my parents' standards. On a weekend
visit away from home with my elder sister, the children of the
house got out cards for a game of 'Beggar my Neighbour'. It
was Sunday and I was horrified. What should I do? Should I
sin with them or, like Ellen in *The Wide Wide World*, rebuke
them and refuse to play. I was too much of a coward, I felt, to
do either. To my great relief my sister, guessing at my dilemma,
managed to whisper to me, 'It would be very rude not to play.'
Another time, when staying with cousins, we actually took a
train on a Sunday. They, too, thought this daring. 'What
would uncle say?' they cried. And I was filled with a guilty joy,
but also with a sort of loyal compunction for though Sunday
observance irked me, yet it provided a sort of security and I did
not like to feel that my parents were being flouted.

Family Prayers and strict Sunday observance were nothing
extraordinary then and did not in themselves do me any harm.
But it was my father's unremitting emotional intensity which
was hard to bear. Not a sunset that was not apocalyptic, not a
bush that was not burning. This intensity was, mercifully,
often lightened by my mother's common sense and irrepress-
ible sense of humour – she was once even known to giggle in
church. We each reacted to our father in different ways: my
elder sister by open rebellion, my brother by evasion, my other
sister by withdrawal, and myself by a period of morbid misery.

It was night-time and I sat up in bed. I was alone, for by this
time my sister was at boarding-school. The moon and stars
were bright and solemn like God and his angels, and I was
afraid of them for I knew that I was wicked. I had told lies and
I did not love my father. I was aware that my parents would be

The author aged four

The author's mother
when young

The author and
her father
at the seaside

The author aged eight, on right, with sister

The family on holiday at Arran

The garden at Oakhampstead, with Pickle the dog

Alfred William Yeo, the author's father, in the drawing room at Oakhampstead, 1916

Dr. K. J. Yeo, the author's brother, in uniform, 1915

The author's room at L.M.H., 1919

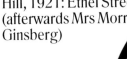
Viva Sunday on Boars
Hill, 1921: Ethel Street
(afterwards Mrs Morris
Ginsberg)

Northcourt House,
Abingdon

The author in 1921

sad and shocked if they knew that I had ever lied. God, of course, already knew. And now the burden of my past lay heavy upon me, for I hadn't seemed of old to mind the odd useful lie, but in the quiet night with the stars watching, I could hear the still small voice of conscience simply shouting at me. Expiation could be granted only through confession. The particular lie that was troubling me so much that night was a singularly harmless one. I had said to my sister that I had read all the books on a certain shelf when I had not. This was not a boast, but it was simply that I did not want to be badgered by her into reading one that she had suggested. Why did this threaten me with hell fire when my real sins lay lightly upon me? I think it was because the children's books that I had read regarded any deviation from the truth as a very grave matter indeed. George Washington was not a joke; the girl or boy who lied always came to a bad end, unless they repented and confessed. That and that alone was my hope.

I opened my door to listen so that I could catch my mother as she came up to bed. It seemed an eternity before I heard her and called, but she came at once and I made my sobbing act of contrition. 'It was a pity,' said my mother, 'but you are sorry now, so don't cry any more but go to sleep.' Bunyan's Christian when his burden fell away could not have felt more exquisitely relieved than I for a moment or two, but then, like a cat with a mouse, my conscience pounced again. Perhaps it wasn't enough to confess to my mother; perhaps I must humble myself before my sister. 'No,' said my mother, 'That isn't necessary. Go to sleep – that is the right thing for you to do now, at this moment.'

The sin of not loving my father could not be expiated by confession, and I did not know what could be done about it. Neither did my poor mother. 'But *he* loves *you* so much,' she said reproachfully, which of course made me feel still more wicked. I knew I did not really love him because I did not want to be with him. I seldom felt at ease with him and it was always a relief when he was not at home. I could not pretend to myself or to my mother that this was not so, for that would be a lie, adding sin to sin. He and God were still mixed up in my mind and I was afraid of and bored by both.

I am sure that my mother never told my father about this trouble, but it was plain that I was morbidly unhappy after my illness and it was decided to send me to the big boarding school where my sister had been. This, as it happened, by providing me with objective miseries, did successfully cure me of self-inflicted ones.

The legacy of my hot-house religious upbringing was an abiding guilt complex. That is its darker side. Set against this are the values implanted by both my parents. Their unworldliness, integrity, and spiritual awareness provided standards for which, however much I fall short of them, I am always grateful.

My comfortable home was, of course, underpinned by servants living under the same roof but quite separate from the family. My father was not wealthy. He did not keep a carriage, relying on Mr Farbrother, who kept stables and provided cabs and Victorias when necessary. Yet we had three maids and a full-time gardener as a matter of course, and these were taken for granted as part of the natural order of things. My mother or aunt did the flowers and a little dusting of the china, but no other housework, and I did not know how to make a bed, wash up, sweep a room, or make a cake when I was married, for I was never taught or required to do these things either at home or at school.

I was not alone in this. In fact at Oxford, unlike my tutor and most of my friends, I did at least know how to boil an egg. My elder sister, who was good at most things, taught herself to cook and could sew beautifully, because she was interested in such pursuits. She had to teach herself, though, as my mother did not really care for such matters and anyway was not a good teacher. She was too impatient, not with us, but with intractable objects. 'Bring it here', 'Never mind, let me see to it for you,' she would cry, too often and too soon.

It was unnecessary for middle and upper class girls to learn homecraft before the 1914 war, for there was always a good supply of servants at a low wage. Every town had its registry offices with plenty of women and girls on their lists, and my mother was never without servants. Behind our green baize door was a pleasant kitchen with a big black-leaded range and a scrubbed deal table and dresser. I was not very familiar with this room as it was ruled over for most of this period by a fierce little elderly cook called Sarah who did not encourage visits. My mother was nervous of Sarah and rarely penetrated into her kitchen; Sarah used to come to her for orders for the day which she would write down on a slate. Adjoining the kitchen was a large scullery (only important to me because my dog's basket was kept there), out of which led a big stone-slabbed larder.

But the room behind the baize door that I knew best was the housemaids' sitting room where the silver and glass were polished. It had an entrance to the yard and the shed where my bicycle lived, and another door to the servants' staircase. When we played hide-and-seek all over the house, this staircase was most useful. Laurie, our housemaid for many years, was my friend and ally. She was brisk and short and had a nice, cheerful, plain face with little, bright, dark eyes rather close together. She left us during the war to get married to an elderly widower. 'But I mean to come and work for you when you're grown up and married yourself, Miss Katharine,' she said when she bid me goodbye, with tears in her little eyes, and I, too, felt like crying.

The young 'between maids', as they were called, came in for the day, arriving early enough in the mornings to lay and light the fires in winter and to set the breakfast table, and staying until after the evening meal. They were always good for a romp when Sarah wasn't about. They changed more often than other maids, leaving to better themselves. There was Ethel, who had lots of little brothers and sisters, and Ursula, who had red hair and a temper, and Maggie, who was fond of telling how, when she was a baby in the pram outside her mother's cottage, a lady came by and was so charmed by her looks that she wanted to adopt her, but her mother, though she had a large family, would not part with her. 'I might have been a lady!' said Maggie wistfully. She had big round eyes and a round rosy face, and had probably been a very pretty baby, but her neck was much too short and she was rather stupid. I preferred Ethel who, like Laurie, was very good-natured and provided an admiring audience when, seated on the table in the housemaid's room, I held forth on every subject under the sun or recited the latest poem I had learnt at school. As a somewhat lonely child, because of being a good deal the youngest, I liked the company of the maids when I could get it, though my mother did not altogether approve, knowing that they spoilt and flattered me.

The maids wore print dresses in the morning and changed in the afternoon into black with white frilly aprons and caps. At Christmas my mother, as was customary, gave them presents of material for these. They had one half-day off a week and alternate Sunday afternoons. Sarah and Laurie slept in the other attic bedroom opposite to my sister's and mine. The first thing I heard in the morning, and the last thing often that I heard at night, was the maids' rustling and bustling down and up the stairs. Sometimes they would talk and laugh too loudly at night, and then my sister or I would get out of bed and knock indignantly on their door and silence would immediately ensue.

My mother kept her maids for years, though I think she was never very easy with them. She was a person who disliked giving orders and was shy, except with her family or a few intimate friends. My father, on the other hand, to whom authority came naturally, always got on well with them and with the gardeners. The first gardener that I remember was a little man whom we called 'Punch'. I don't know what his real name was. My mother was a keen gardener and loved flowers. 'I don't like those colours together, we must plant that bed differently next year,' she said once to Punch. 'Why, Ma'am, I think they clash beautiful,' he said. Then there was Absalom (that really was his name). He was a crank and brought up his children on a diet mainly of bananas and milk, to my mother's disapproval: 'Poor little things, they are much too fat.' Lastly there was William, younger than the others and, like Laurie, my special friend. He contrived hutches out of boxes for my rabbits and sowed my name in mustard and cress in a corner of the vegetable garden. He, too, was treated to a recital of my favourite stories and poems, as I sat comfortably among the trays of sweet-smelling apples and drying herbs in his nice wooden shed.

The garden produced quite enough fruit and vegetables to feed us, and this was no small quantity, for the gong summoned the family to four solid meals each day. We should have scorned a breakfast that did not provide eggs and bacon, or haddock, or kidneys, as well as porridge and toast and marmalade; then there was elevenses, tea and biscuits (milk if one was young), followed by a substantial lunch of two courses, which was my dinner. Tea at four o'clock consisted of bread and butter (white, for brown was very little known) and home-make cakes, and in winter dripping toast or muffins bought from the muffin man who came to the door ringing a hand-bell and carrying the muffins on a tray on his head. Dinner at night, for the 'grown ups' was usually of three courses and dessert – no wine of course but often home-made lemonade.

Food was cheap and plentiful and all home-cooked. Everybody who could afford it probably ate too much, but on the other hand they took more exercise. My father walked to and from the station every day (about two and a half miles), unless it was very wet when he had a cab from Mr Farbrother. We walked to school, and my mother walked to the shops or to visit her friends: the roads and streets were full of walkers. Even our quiet road had constant foot travellers: besides the muffin man there was the 'rag and bone man', the 'chairs to mend' man, the 'knives to grind' man, and sometimes a Punch and Judy show, not to speak of all the usual callers and tradesmen.

Besides eating more and walking more, we wore more

clothes. When, as a little child, I used to be taken for walks, I remember tucking my hand into the crook made by my mother's or aunt's hands as they held up long, voluminous skirts and petticoats. Grandmothers always wore caps and shawls, and widows had caps with long streamers and yards of crepe on their black dresses, for mourning was universally observed, near relatives wearing black for at least a year before they were allowed grey or mauve. Jays of Regent Street used to sell nothing but mourning; I peered at their windows with morbid interest. Everyone, young and old, men and women, boys and girls, wore hats or bonnets or caps. I remember poor children in the London streets with no shoes and stockings, but never without something on their heads. There were top hats and bowlers and straw boaters and all sorts of caps for the men, and women had whole gardens or aviaries on their heads.

Our clothes were warm and heavy in the winter, for houses were colder and trains, carriages, and cabs were cold too. My first journey alone by train was in winter. The train was not heated at all but I had a long, flat, hot water container provided to keep my feet warm. I was met at the station by a governess cart and pony, and when I got to the end of my journey I was able to thaw out before a glowing fire in my bedroom.

Even in summer people, especially women, wore a lot of clothes: stiffly starched cotton or linen long skirts and blouses with high necks, beneath which were petticoats and camisoles and stays and long knickers and vests, or combination. Only in very hot weather were any of these discarded. Even bathing dresses had to have skirts for women and were long in the legs for men. Sunbathing was unheard of; in fact our bodies were mostly quite invisible and unfamiliar even to ourselves.

But though we all wore more clothes at a time, we had fewer of them and what we had were made to last and colours and patterns were restricted. Gradually, as I grew older, skirts became a little shorter and bodices looser. The aesthetic movement had spread since the 'greenery yallery Grosvenor Gallery' days and was now having a wider influence. Liberty's, in Regent Street, represented for us the height of loveliness. To wander in the rooms and corridors of this famous shop was like exploring Aladdin's cave. All the same, when emerging into the streets again one day and hailing a bus which duly drew up for us (as they did then wherever one happened to be), my mother remarked, 'It's rather a relief, don't you think, to see a solid vulgar red omnibus after all that good taste.'

The pleasure of climbing to the top of an open bus and forging your way to a front seat was great. It was like being in the prow of a ship. If it rained there was a tarpaulin cover at hand to button you snuggly in, and you put up your umbrella, and there you were, watching a fascinating pool of water collecting on your tarpaulin lap. The joy of open bus rides was only equalled by a hansom cab when you were shut in by folding wooden flaps and, safe in this smaller craft, went swaying along behind the horse's tail.

At Liberty's my mother had bought a length of material to make me a summer frock. It was to be made up for me by Miss Blanche Worsefold, our dressmaker (we seldom had ready-made dresses). She lived with her sister in a tiny stuffy house and I don't believe either of them ever went outside if they could help it; they were pale like little ghosts. You rang the bell and the sister always answered it and said, without a pause in one breath, 'Will-you-come-in-please-will-you-sit-down-please-Blanchey-Blanchey-you're-wanted.' I never knew anyone who could put as many pins in her mouth at once as Blanchey.

To have a new dress was an event, and I loved that one, which was of a soft blue and green silk. It was to be my best for some years until I went to boarding school and had to have a whole new outfit. It went with me on the last summer holiday of freedom which was spent on the Devonshire coast with my cousins (Barbellion's family). The next year I had experienced my first traumatic term away from home and everything was different, and the year after that was the summer of 1914. But this year the waves break innocently upon the great golden beaches where I ride a little chestnut pony along the hard sand.

When I have saved up enough money or cajoled some from my father, I can hire him for long enough to shake off the other inferior ponies and the contemptible donkeys and trot away into the exciting solitary distance. My ambition to own a rocking-horse (never realized) had become by this time a longing for a real pony (also never realized), but in this timeless moment this is my own pony and I continued for years to ride him in my dreams.

Altogether that was a happy summer, for on that seaside holiday my elder sister became engaged to one of these Devonshire cousins. There were three brothers. 'Which of them do you like best?' enquired my sister of me just before things came to a head. I said the wrong one. Not that I wasn't fond of all three of them, but Bruce (W.N.P. Barbellion), who was my choice, had lived with us while he was working up for a post at the Natural History Museum, and he was the most interesting person I had ever known, though I knew he was not always kind.

This holiday provided a neat parallel insect story to my Arran earwig one. This time it was a huge spider suspended over my bed in our lodgings. I was, as usual, dispatched to my room long before the others and I sat hugging my knees until I heard Bruce springing up the stairs. I called to him and he came but, unlike my brother, *not* to my aid. He sat on the edge of my bed and lectured me. I was, he said, 'a very silly little girl,' nothing like so clever or beautiful as the spider whose life history I was then forced to hear at some length. Eventually he said goodnight and left me alone with the spider. On that same holiday, however, he took me deep sea fishing, not ordinary fishing but a naturalist's fishing which meant dredging with a net, examining the contents, and then carefully restoring them again.

My sister got engaged among the rocks and sea pools and I was busy spying, not on her but on sea anemones and little crabs, when I came upon her and my cousin. They were kissing. 'We are going to get married,' they said and I was very pleased. The next day we all went for an expedition and my sister admired a set of Meredith's novels in red leather displayed in a bookshop window. Harry, my cousin, immediately bought them for her. This impressed me greatly, much more than the kissing. It was being treated like a princess.

Home once again where the late summer flowers were burning themselves out in the garden; my mother, walking between the two hedges of sweet peas (her favourite flower), picked the last of them regretfully, but the roses were still blooming and the dahlias and michaelmas daisies would soon be here to comfort her. The garden had been my schoolroom all that summer, for I was still supposed to be delicate after my rheumatic fever. I had no regular lessons but had quite enjoyed reading Tartaran de Turascon with my sister who was a good linguist, and I had kept a Nature Note Book. I had also, under the influence of *A Secret Garden*, cultivated my own plot and had tried to make friends with a robin.

I was not to go to my big final school until the winter was over, but it was arranged that, in order to break me in to being away from home, I should go as a weekly boarder to a small private school in the neighbourhood. It did nothing of the sort for Thornton House was in every possible way the antithesis of what awaited me at Wycombe Abbey. Even in those days it was something of an anachronism. It was kept by two elderly maiden ladies; Miss Wood and Miss Walker. Miss Wood was handsome and majestic with piled white hair, Miss Walker was small, lively and practical, and I never saw either of them ever anything but serene. Miss Wood taught Scripture and Miss Walker French, and everything else except Botany and Art was taught by another elderly spinster, Miss Hall, who I don't think had any qualifications other than unfailing patience and affection for us all. The standard of work was low. With my sound High School foundation it was quite easy for me to top the weekly class lists with very little exertion. There was a visiting mistress for Botany which, as in Victorian days, was an important branch of feminne education. Drawing and dancing and dreadful 'barbola' work was also taught. For this last you had a special pen and decorated inoffensive mats and traycloths with butterflies and roses blobbed on to the material with oily paints. I loved doing this even more than I had loved making sealing wax hat pins. The school was housed in two adjoining small Edwardian villas, and had only a patch of garden which no one seemed to use. There were no organized games, and for exercise we were taken for daily walks by Miss Hall, walking in a crocodile, two by two. Our ages ranged from six or seven to fifteen years, and there were about twenty boarders and perhaps as many day pupils.

I was happy at Thornton House. I think this was partly because it was more like one of my storybook schools come to life than a real school and this charmed me. We even had a midnight feast once, only it wasn't midnight and Miss Wood and Miss Walker knew all about it and provided a cake. No-one now would believe in us. When the day girls had departed, we settled down like a large family and this too, for me, had the fascination of a dream realized. We played family games and, after the little ones had gone to bed, we elders followed our own various pursuits until it was half past eight when we filed into Miss Wood's and Miss Walker's room to receive a goodnight kiss and a sweet. We slept in rooms of three or four beds and were allowed to talk till nine o'clock. My bed was next to a nice girl called Olive who put out her hand to touch me comfortingly on the first night, in case I should be lonely. She had a three-cornered patch of bright blue in one of her large brown eyes and a face like a Leonardo painting.

I lost no time in making friends at Thornton House. Olive and I started a magazine and organized complicated charades. I enjoyed my weekends at home too, finding this counterpoint between school and home invigorating rather than disturbing, and my mother was relieved for it seemed as though I was going to take to boarding school. The trouble was that it was not like a real boarding school in the least. We had our squabbles and our silliness, of course, but no more than those of an ordinary, large, healthy, varied family. It was a friendly, cheerful place and I did not stay there long enough for the low educational standards to become boring. For the present I was quite content; both heaven and hell had temporarily receded during this improbable interlude, leaving me for a short space in Eden. I learnt nothing of consequence there any more than did Adam and Eve until they were turned out into the real world, but it was certainly enjoyable.

CHAPTER FIVE

1913–1916
Boarding school

The chestnut trees bordering the fields where the Jersey cows lived were bursting into leaf, the lilac was out, and I was going for a last evening walk with my sister. My trunk was packed, and laid out in my room were my first ever coat and skirt, navy as required by the clothes list, but with a natty patent leather belt and a lining of shot peacock blue and green silk. Tomorrow I was to set off for my third and final and largest and most important school.

My dear parents had made one miscalculation in supposing that Thornton House would prepare me for the Abbey; now they made another. Thinking it would be better for my health to start this new life in the summer, they dispatched me at the end of the school year so that I was the only new girl in my House and my form.

The choice of House was also unfortunate. There were eight Houses, four in the main building and four 'out houses' climbing the steep hill. Again, because of health, they chose the highest and the furthest away from the low-lying Abbey with its lake. There was another reason, though, for a Scotch Presbyterian Minister had sent his daughter to that same House: 'She will be a nice friend for you.' Actually she was older, higher up the school, and hardly spoke a word to me. What my parents also did not realize was that the house mistress, one of the original staff that had started the school, was now past her best (she retired the year after) and that as a consequence the house was not in a particularly healthy condition in spite of its position. Or it may have been that it happened just then to contain a few undesirable girls, two of whom were later required to leave.

I think I would have been a little less unhappy had I been in one of the other Houses, though this is uncertain, for the whole system under which the school was run was, I believe, unnatural. It was founded, together with other similar schools, at a time when there was a popular movement towards going one better (so it was thought) than the High Schools and providing for girls the equivalent of the boys' great public schools. It was an asset if, like so many of the latter, the actual buildings could lay claim to some beauty and tradition. The Abbey only dated back to the Gothic revival of the late 18th and early 19th centuries, but it was dignified and gracious. Pitt had stayed there when the lime trees in the avenue were first planted and it possessed a fine hall, staircase, library, and cloisters. It must have been one of the first country houses to be turned into a school. Of course, when it was taken over, much had been added in the way of boarding accommodation and classrooms. 'This stone was laid in 1898', I used to read resentfully when I passed a certain corner. It was the year of my birth; how could Fate be so cruel!

The cult of tradition, 'esprit de corps', and athleticism had been taken over lock, stock, and barrel – indeed, like most convents, we went even further than our models in some directions. There were no studies and we had little time to ourselves; in fact we had absolutely no privacy and no leisure time at all except on Sunday afternoons in summer. 'Satan finds some mischief for idle hands to do' seemed to have been engraved on the hearts of our founders. From the time when the maids came round, sloshing the cold water into our tin baths in the mornings, till the head of the dormitory extinguished our lights at night, we were running round in a crowd to the sound of bells.

There were lots of little rules that implied lack of trust in the individual. No-one was allowed into the town except with a visiting parent, all letters addressed to anyone but our parents had to be enclosed in one to them, friendships with older girls were discouraged, and, for some reason or other, even friendships with members of other houses were not looked upon favourably. This reduced the choice of friends to a very small compass. A strict hierarchy was observed and there were many unwritten laws to catch out the unwary (for instance, woe betide the girl who took a seat in the House study unbefitting her exact position in House order, even though that seat might be vacant). But above all it was the importance of compulsory games that was predominant in such schools. No single subject, none of the arts and certainly no hobby, took up so much time and energy, nor claimed such regard. If one was no good at running after a ball, one was no good.

But my mother and I were innocent of all this as we travelled down together from Paddington on that May morning. I was self-confident and excited. In the train I practised tying my school tie, to the amusement of an old gentleman opposite, for I made a poor job of it. My mother and I were also amused, though really the muddle I made was not a matter for amusement at all. It could have been, if we had known it, a symbol of my inadequacy in the face of all that that tie stood for.

On arrival we were given tea by the plump, elderly house mistress, and then I was actually quite glad to say goodbye to my mother, so eager was I to begin my new life. I found my trunk standing in a row with others in the cloakroom, where all around girls were busy unpacking their things into round wicker clothes-baskets which they carried upstairs. I looked about but I could not see where they got these baskets and I did not know where to go or what to do. I accosted one of the girls but she brushed me aside. I tried again, but I might have been invisible. A quiver of dismay assailed me, as yet hardly acknowledged, but at last someone noticed me and showed me where to get one of those mysterious baskets. She told me to lay out all my clothes upon my bed for checking with the clothes list. My cubicle was the least desirable in the house, being a passage way to the rest of the dormitory and thus lacking any privacy, which horrified me. My apparent invisibility also perplexed me all through the rest of the day, but I told myself that all would be well when everyone had settled down and life would be splendid.

I did not sleep well, however; I was cold and someone snored and in the morning I was slow getting up and dealing with my hip bath. We all had tin hip baths under our beds and were allowed one very small can of hot water each; otherwise cold baths every morning were the rule. There was too little time left for my tie and, as I finished with it, I thought of the old gentleman who had smiled at me in the train – it was a memory of what already seemed a different and kinder world.

To reassure myself I decided to wear the hair ribbons that were my mother's favourite colour. My bushy and very curly hair was her pride and she had selected these ribbons herself. They were pale blue. I hastily tied them on and ran down the stairs, the last to leave the dormitory. The brisk little matron stood at the door of the dining room to check up on every girl as she went in, and when she saw me she frowned. 'Haven't you got some navy or black hair ribbons?' she asked. I blushed and mumbled that I had. 'Then run up quickly and change them' she said. I ran, hot with sorrow and shame. My mother had thought these so pretty and, if I had blundered so to begin with, what lay in wait for me during the rest of the day?

Hurry, hurry, hurry – after breakfast it was all a rush and then hundreds of faces in a huge hall. Above me on the platform was the headmistress, like no other that I had met, for she was quite young and looked like an archangel or 'Tiger, tiger burning bright', she was so awesome and beautiful, and so far removed from ordinary life. Her voice was low-pitched but extremely clear as she gave out the school hymn, 'Through the night of doubt and sorrow'. It seemed to me very appropriate and the psalm that followed was 'I will lift up mine eyes unto the hills from whence cometh my help'. But where were those hills of God? They seemed to me very far off that day and for many days to come.

The hills round the school were covered in beech woods and from my seat at the House study table I could look out on them and on the smooth green slope beneath. In the mornings the shadows stretched out on this slope towards the west and seemed to threaten the long dismal day ahead. Then, when evening came and they had moved round to the east, I eagerly crossed off another square on the calendar I had made at the back of my rough notebook.

I was not a success. 'What do you think you're doing?' 'Oh, she's hopeless!' 'Run, can't you, run!' 'You're a disgrace to the House.' Everything about me was wrong. I looked untidy, my wretched tie never neat, my blouse often parting company with my skirt. I had a long back and not much in the way of hips, and my mother had thought to get over the difficulty of a tuck-in blouse (for elastic ones were not allowed) by sewing press buttons on, but these continually snapped apart and became a source of ridicule. So did the lovely lining and belt of my coat because it was different. And so, oh shame upon shame, were my sweets.

Sweets were given in to a common hoard, of which the matron was custodian. Twice a week she gave out the amount she thought proper to the owner, who then passed them round to everyone after lunch. Everybody but myself seemed to have great glorious boxes of chocolates, but I had only three paper bags full of toffee. It was an almond toffee of which I was particularly fond; but, alas, it had never occurred to my mother or myself that this would be kept in a cupboard until eventually shared out, by which time it would have irretrievably stuck to the miserable little bags. When at length they were produced, I was too ashamed to claim them. 'Who do these belong to?' asked Matron. There was no answer. 'Well,' she said, after a dreadful pause, 'They are terribly sticky. I'm afraid I must throw them away.'

There seemed no end to my blunders and incompetence, but all would have been forgiven if I had been able to play a decent game of cricket. However, fate had decreed otherwise – she had not given me the right kind of arms and legs for cricket. I was quite good at swimming and croquet, but neither of these were catered for here. Not that I had the chance for weeks to take part in an actual game; the whole of every afternoon was spent in standing in a line and having cricket balls slung at me to train the eye and harden the hands. As I ran after the ball, invariably missed, the grass verges of the pitch, thick with buttercups and moondaisies, mocked me with their beauty. The school grounds were unbearably lovely, with a lake and a long lime avenue, but in this harried life how could they be enjoyed? 'Hurry up now. You might at least try!' 'For goodness sake what are your hands *made* of?'

There were, of course, some mitigations for my unhappiness. There were letters, though to read them I usually retreated to the lavatories, the only place safe from intrusion, for, though precious, they often reduced me to tears. My mother wrote very often and my father not infrequently. I had loving letters from dear Thornton House, and my cousin Bruce wrote offering to elope with me. I knew he did not mean it but it comforted me. In an orgy of self-indulgent misery I wrote my own letters home every Sunday and Thursday and eased my heart a little.

Then there was *The Moonstone* by Wilkie Collins. This was read to the younger ones by the house mistress while their elders were doing the late evening's period of prep. It was almost civilized to sit on a comfortable chair in the drawing-room, and the house mistress read well. For a brief period Mr Collins banished my griefs. Afterwards came prayers and blessed bed and, before lights went off, I read each night a passage from *Evening Thoughts*, a small devotional book given me by my mother on the day I left home. I did this at first because I felt it to be a link with her, but then, soon and unexpectedly, I began to find in the words themselves comfort and reassurance. Sundays too were transformed, for here they were the only days on which there was even a semblance of leisure. In the morning before the service, for instance, there was 'Silent Hour', when one was actually required to sit still and read a suitable book. Luckily, Victorian classical novels were considered suitable, but Charlotte Bronte's *Villette* was not perhaps a happy choice as I identified too easily with homesick, lonely, self-pitying Lucy Snow. The sense of rejection and inadequacy was an entirely new and bewildering experience for me, but I was not altogether cowed. I resolved to write a novel and to portray in a lurid light the girls I most disliked. That would teach them!

We had no half-term holiday, but every first Thursday in the month was Visiting Day from lunchtime till after tea. My mother never failed me on these days, nor did it ever occur to me that she could. I waited with others at the main gate. One or two motorcars drew up in splendour, to everyone's admiration, but nearly every visitor arrived by train and proceeded on their legs from the station to the school where, after a rapturous greeting, the were immediately walked off again in search of a meal. There were only two available places in the town for this: the Red Lion Hotel for the swells and an unpretentious tea shop-cum-restaurant for the rest. I would steer my mother into the furthest corner of this. It had been good to see in the street beings other than girls and mistresses – old people and babies, men and boys, dogs and cats, all going happily about their business – but the restaurant was stuffed with girls again and as soon as lunch was over we would retreat into the side lanes where I could weep unseen. It must have been jolly for my mother.

Visiting Days were full of joy and pain. As the afternoon wore on the shadow of parting lay heavily upon me. One time, as I ran blindly back from the gate, I nearly bumped into the headmistress who was apparently relieving her feelings after a surfeit of parents by weeding the drive. 'Don't you think it would be a good idea to try and cheer up?' she asked me. I was speechless – it was the first time she had spoken personally to me. I nodded agreement. What else could one do to an archangel? But I failed to take her advice, which only deepened my sense of alienation, though she meant it kindly. In fact all the staff that I encountered were kind. There were only two horrors. One was a niece of the redoubtable Miss Buss of 19th-century pioneering fame, who was very handsome, very fierce, and very capricious; the other was the head of the music staff. But I never came under the sway of either. Lessons were a refuge and provided a modicum of self-respect, not that they mattered as much as games, of course.

The curriculum was much the same as that of the High

School, for, though there was a lab, the one period a week of elementary chemistry, taught by the geography mistress, was not taken very seriously. This was partly because she was no disciplinarian, and the time was passed pleasantly in diversions such as trying to roast potatoes over the Bunsen burners. Art was an extra and I cannot recall it playing any part at all in the lives of those who did not 'take it'.

Instrumental music was also an extra. There were several piano mistresses graded according to cost, and my parents, eager as usual to do the best they could for me, chose the most expensive but one. She was obsessed with technique and treated all her pupils as if they were budding professionals. They had to spend a great deal of time doing finger exercises before they even touched the keys, and pieces were learnt very accurately and by memory. But alas, no sight reading was encouraged. Still, she was better than the most expensive one, who was very large and terrible. There was a dreadful institution about three times a term called 'Musical Evening', when various victims had to perform before the whole school, whose attendance was obligatory. The head music mistress would enliven the atmosphere by shouting out her approbation or, more often, disapproval. 'Take that again more slowly', 'Don't stumble', 'Go back and start again'.

There was a school orchestra of sorts, but the main musical activity was directed towards the all-pervading House competitive spirit. The singing cup was given every summer and it mattered how your House did in the competition – oh, how it mattered! The song chosen by my House that first dismal term was *The Ash Grove*, the tune of which has ever since seemed to me intolerably mournful. But apart from this competition, we had one singing session every week. Each Wednesday morning there appeared on the platform at School Prayers a small, pale, rather comic-looking man who made the piano sound altogether different. We always had *For all the Saints* on Wednesdays, and Vaughan Williams's lovely tune (written not long before) resounded to the accompaniment of intriguing, spontaneous trimmings. Mr Holst remained after prayers were over

67

and took classes throughout the day. We had no idea that he was a great composer (he was then engaged on *The Planets*). We were too ignorant and too conventional to appreciate him anyway, and I am sure he did not like us much. St Paul's, the other girls' school he taught, knew better, and it was for them he wrote the *St Paul's Suite*. We certainly did not compare well with them in his eyes. He appeared to us merely an oddity and I am ashamed to say that when war broke out a rumour was started that he was a German spy. All the same, some of us at any rate couldn't help being impressed by his vitality and enthusiasm. I can see him now shaking his fist at us as we feebly wavered through *Scots w' hae wi Wallace bled*. 'Think what you're saying,' he shouted. 'Think! You're facing the hateful English for your lives' sake, your children, your homes. "See approach proud Edward's power', see it, see it!' He danced about the platform. 'Chains and slavery,' he snarled ferociously. But chains and slavery were all we were good for.

Singing song after song (mostly public school favourites) on the last night of term needed no exhortation and went with real gusto:

> Forty years on when afar and asunder
> Parted are those that are singing today.

Well, I wouldn't have to wait forty years for that, thank goodness: only twelve hours, for the school train left early. I had not believed it when I saw my old, friendly trunk again waiting for me in the cloakroom on that packing-day morning. I think I had feared that I would never see it again and I could hardly sleep for excitement. But the night passed, the day came, and my mother was waiting for me at the end of the journey. When we actually reached home I ran upstairs to take off my things. I went to the window; below me the garden stretched out in a bright pattern of high summer flowers, but they shimmered and sparkled in rainbow colours for I was seeing them through tears. It is the only time I can remember crying for joy. My mother's voice called up at me to come down, for friends were waiting to see me. I dabbed at my eyes and ran out into the sun.

Time turned a somersault during the holidays. At school each day had seemed an eternity, dragging its slow length painfully along, but now it rushed past. I had nightmares in which I was back in that alien hostile world and, waking, was not comforted because I knew it was there waiting for me and I was one day nearer to it. Just as I had spoiled the last hours of visiting days by thoughts of the inevitable parting ahead, so the last week of my time at home was ruined by miserable forebodings. I was reading *The Scarlet Pimpernel* and the taxi that took me from Charing Cross to Paddington on the final morning seemed to me just like a tumbril on its way to the guillotine. I choked over the last meal in the elegant, dignified station restaurant with its attentive waitress, that at that time graced Platform 1 at Paddington. At the last possible moment I stumbled into a carriage of the school train, which was full of vociferous clamour. I shrank into a corner, and prepared for the worst.

The worst, however, didn't happen, for things were perceptively improved this term. First there were a number of new girls, and therefore I was no longer the dregs; indeed in their eyes, until they knew better, I was as good as anyone else. Then I was moved up a form and lessons were more interesting. Lacrosse too I found a less impossible game than cricket, and there were even people who were worse at it than myself. Lastly and most important, as the weeks went by, I saw a dawning possibility of making a special friend.

Special friends were called 'Better Halves' and were indispensable. There was a strict convention that you had to have one and when you were paired off you were expected to sit, walk, and talk with your Better Half and with no other unless one of you was absent for some reason. Lacking a Better Half, you were either forced into the company of other outcasts or back on yourself, which was the ultimate shame. This had been my condition all that first term, but now I hardly dared tell myself, someone who had previously made a misalliance (for such things did happen) was actually making advances towards me.

It was almost unbelievable, for she was good at lacrosse and quite popular. But, though she could run very fast, she was not 'gamey'. Her name was Grace, and she was sensible, good natured, and liked history. She was fair and red-cheeked with pale fierce blue eyes, a thin beaky nose, and long thin legs. She looked rather like a bird. By the end of the term it was almost understood that she and I were Better Halves.

But I was still often very homesick and there were still many things and some people I hated, and I certainly did not minimize these in my letters home. I think I was almost afraid to dwell on any gleams of light in case they should vanish. I looked forward as eagerly as ever to the holidays, especially as there was Christmas also ahead to be enjoyed.

This time, to save my mother the very early start to meet the school train, my brother had offered to be her deputy until she could call for me later. He was now a medical student at the London Hospital and lived with a friend in rooms in Marylebone Road. There we drove from the station and when we arrived the nice landlady had provided a second breakfast for me (there was no such thing then as students' flats or any question of them doing for themselves). This was all an added glory to the day, and when my mother arrived to take me Christmas shopping I was in a state of exalted bliss. My mother too seemed extra happy. 'You've kept your promise, you haven't told her?' she said mysteriously to my brother. 'What is it?' I asked. 'A piece of good news for you,' said my mother. 'You're not going back to the Abbey next term. It's all arranged, you're going to a very nice small school at Eastbourne instead where I'm sure you'll be much happier. There, darling!'

I was dumbfounded and then suddenly overcome with fury. This reaction took all three of us by surprise, for during this whole episode I seem to have been swept along by some force of which I was only half aware and over which I had little control. Two emotions were uppermost; first, anger that such a momentous decision had been taken without consulting me, that everything had been settled behind my back, and secondly, dismay that just as I was beginning to win through, I was to be removed forcibly from the battlefield. Had all my misery been for nothing, then? I determined on the spot that this couldn't be allowed. 'But you are so unhappy!' exclaimed my mother. 'I know, I know,' I sobbed, for I was overcome now by excitement, fatigue, and shock. 'But it doesn't matter so much, it doesn't matter. I don't *want* to go to another school, I *won't* go to another school.' 'Oh dear, oh dear!' said my mother. 'I'm sure you'll think differently when you hear what a lovely school it is, and it can't be helped now,' she added with a justifiable note of exasperation in her voice, for she too had had a shock. My brother said, 'Try not to think anything more about it for the present anyway, or you'll spoil the day.' But the day that had promised so much glory was already irretrievably flawed, though I went off with my mother to do the Christmas shopping trying to do as my brother had said.

During the days that followed, my parents argued with me in vain. The alluring prospectus of Belmont which they gave me to read had no effect, the only slight temptation being that it had longer holidays – a whole week longer at Christmas. That made me hesitate, but only for a short time. At night, before I slept, I saw very clearly, bright before me, the Lime Avenue, the little island in the lake, the big cedars, the humped beech trees on the hills, and the grey buildings of the Abbey itself. How sad that they would go on being beautiful, but never for me again. On the last night of the term it was the custom for every member of the staff to shake hands with each girl and, on that final farewell which I did not know was final the Archangel, I remembered now, had given me a specially solemn and penetrating look. I had wondered momentarily about this, but of course she was dismissing me as a miserable defeatist. As I lay in my bed I also thought of my newly-acquired Better Half with an empty seat beside her once more. Full of drama and woe, which was not wholly unenjoyable, at last I slept.

I got my own way in the end. My parents reluctantly agreed to write to the Abbey to find out whether my place had yet been filled and whether they could withdraw their notice. It hadn't been and they could. 'What I can say to Belmont I really don't know,' said my poor mother.

At the beginning of the next term the headmistress sent for me. I went in fear and trembling; it was only the second time she had spoken to me individually. 'Now tell me what made you come back?' she asked. I gazed out of the great mullioned Gothic window of her room to the wide stretch of green turf beyond. 'I didn't want to go to a silly little private school,' I said. It was a diplomatic though quite unpremeditated reply and it met with approval. She laughed, 'Well, I'm glad you are here anyway,' she said, 'and I'm sure you won't regret it.'

She was right, for my answer, even if suspiciously apt and only one out of several I might have given, was truly how I felt, though I did not exactly know why. I think I equated Belmont and all private schools with dear but very limited Thornton House, and I was right in that it would never have occurred to me had I gone there even to have tried for Oxford, and Oxford was to be of great importance to me. But apart from this, to have left the Abbey at that point would have been a muddle and I have never liked loose ends and not finishing things. I believe though, that if, at the end of my first term the same proposition had been made, I might well have jumped at it. As it was, with my secure home background, the unhappiness I had experienced did me no real harm; in fact it was probably good for me. For one thing, it gave me some little idea of what if felt like to be despised and outcast, though I think the system did harm some. Later I met several girls from other similar public schools who had suffered equally. Perhaps we were all birds of a feather. We were fully recompensed, however, by the keenness of the contrasting pleasure with which we savoured the freedom and friendliness we found at Oxford.

CHAPTER SIX

1914–1918
War years

It was the beginning of August 1914 and once again I was home for the summer holidays and looking forward to travelling to Scotland the very next day. My brother had just qualified and had chosen our destination, Nairn on the east coast, because of its famous golf course. He, my father, and myself were together under the oak tree. It was a perfect evening and I was lazily swinging to and fro on the old swing listening to the others talking, but their conversation was far from being as peaceful as the weather.

The Archduke Ferdinand of Austria had been assassinated, an event which had not troubled me in the least, but now it appeared that Austria and Germany, France and Russia were all going to make war because of this. The latest news which I had not taken in before was that because Germany threatened to march through Belgium on their way to Paris, we would have to fight too. It was, however, not until I heard my brother speak one brief sentence that I began even dimly to realize what this meant. I can hear his troubled voice still: 'If there is war it will put back civilization a hundred years or more, no matter what happens.' My father, optimistic as always, said: 'I put my trust in Grey. Germany will never risk antagonizing us.' But when the next morning the papers told us that inconceivably, war had actually been declared, most of us believed that our Navy would protect us from all real harm, that our Army would acquit itself gloriously, and that it would soon be over. 'No country can afford to go to war for long nowadays,' said my father.

We did not think for a moment of abandoning our holiday, but the hitherto unimaginable fact of war was at once apparent to us, for the platforms and trains were full of soldiers and bewildered, excited people.

We were to break our journey at Edinburgh and we put up at a hotel facing the Castle. This in itself was deeply romantic and now, against this splendid background, history was coming alive before my eyes as I stood at a window and watched a Highland regiment swinging along down Princes Street to the sound of bagpipes. My brother's prophetic forebodings faded away and I was filled with excitement. But some of the Highland officers were staying at our hotel and there was one with a young wife who had a table next to us that evening. How sad and silent they were. As I looked at them, some dim sense of tragedy invaded me and this double vision of glory and grief stayed with me throughout at least the early period of the war.

Fear did not enter in, not even when we learned as much as we were allowed to be told of the Allies' initial defeats, for I had been too firmly preconditioned to security. Soon, though, I was made to understand that the war could affect me personally, though as yet in a very minor and indirect way. My brother only had two days at Nairn before he was recalled to go on duty at the London Hospital. After his departure the holiday fell to pieces.

There were only four of us left, as my elder sister had got married that spring. I had been a bridesmaid in a daffodil yellow silk dress and a picture hat tied under my chin. I had felt uncertain of myself and tried to be amusing and grown-up and helpful, and to hide the blow my cousin Bruce dealt me that day with his occasional characteristic cruelty. He said: 'You've grown to be just like any other school girl – I'm not interested in you any more.' He was busy at the time falling in love with the 'E'* of his *Diary*, but I did not know this. Still, I had managed to enjoy myself at the wedding. It was a beautiful

* My favourite cousin Eleanor

April day and the gathering of friends and relations a splendid one, as befitted a last party of an epoch that was drawing to its end, only no-one knew it to be so. Now, at dismal Nairn, my remaining sister and I tried to comfort each other, but it was cold and grey. We hired bicycles and explored the country around, but this was not a patch on Arran and the sea was icy. We were glad when it was time to go home.

By this time refugees from brave little Belgium were sprinkled about the country and the Belgian flag was much in evidence. The refugees wore black and looked understandably glum, and there were parties to try and cheer them up. The mood of glory still being uppermost in me, I got up one day before breakfast to bicycle to Reigate Heath to cheer the Surrey regiment marching past on their way to Dover. I also drew a picture of St George and the Dragon and illuminated an exhortation by Alfred Noyes or Sir Henry Newbolt or perhaps somebody else:

> England what thou wert, thou art,
> Gird thee with thine ancient might,
> Faith and God protect the right.

This my father framed and hung beside his desk. But the news during that September was grave, for all the gloss the newspapers put on it, and myths had to be invented to boost our morale. I should like to have believed in the Angel who turned back the Germans after Mons was taken, and in the Russian troops with snow on their boots that a great many people saw travelling the length of Britain to be transported to France to save the day, but I couldn't quite manage it. What, however, I did unquestionably believe in, was that our Army and Navy were invincible and could never in the end be beaten.

Back at school I wrote a patriotic poem, not perhaps up to Rupert Brook, but breathing a like spirit of exultation. I can remember the first verse still:

> Called the white cliffs of Dover to the white cliffs of
>   France
> Across the darkening waters of the sea.
> Sister oh my sister are you yet awake?
> Or do the restless billows that foam around you make
> An unresisted lullaby for thee?

Probably the rest of it matched, but I'm glad to say the school magazine refused it. I was surprised but not mortified by the rejection.

Everyone still hoped the war would be over by Christmas. But it was not, and it was then that my brother told us he felt he must enlist for service abroad. He joined the RAMC and was appointed as Captain in the Royal York and Lancaster regiment home from India and about to embark for France. He had had, of course, no experience whatever of the forces, and felt very young and alien to all those seasoned Regular Army officers. He went to join them at Winchester in the New Year where there was to be a big gathering of troops and a special service for them and their relatives in the Cathedral.

Term had begun, but I was given leave to go with my parents to stay in Winchester for the weekend. The Cathedral was quite full and the beauty of the place, the music, and the gathered emotion of that grieving and glorying congregation were intense. I never thought how similar services were at that same time taking place in Germany, presumably appealing to the same God – the God of Hosts. I was full of pride in my brother in his Captain's uniform, but I was full too of heartache at the parting. There were flags everywhere and bands playing, as at Edinburgh, but now everything was grimmer and people were beginning to talk of a longer and a harder war than they had at first thought possible. At Winchester we had lodgings in a little ancient house in the High Street. It was a bitterly cold January and the streets were thick with snow and quite silent and deserted except for the troops going by. Early on the morning after the service I lay in my huge feather bed in my tiny room and listened to the dull,

76

thudding sound of their boots marching past in the snow, rank after rank marching on into the distance.

At first my brother's letters were pretty cheerful, though conveying a general impression of noise, mud, and muddle. His battalion was sent to relieve the French near Ypres. All place-names were left blank but we gathered the vicinity from various hints.

Apparently for once the Germans did not know we had arrived to take over, for the next day they threw a note over into our trenches, only about fifteen yards away. I saw it, it was written in very good French which said: 'We have no quarrel with you, join with us against the British'.

The guns have been a little quieter this morning and I managed to get some rest, but I suppose they will start again soon. At the time of the shelling one hates it but I am glad to say that if there is a peaceful interval one soon forgets one's troubles. In the intervals between the noise of the guns one can hear the larks singing.

His job was to establish a dressing station somewhere in a ruined house or a barn, which only too frequently had to be abandoned and a fresh one set up. As spring advanced the fighting became more active and came to a head in his part of the line at the battle of Ypres, when the Germans used poison gas for the first time. My mother sent me on my brother's letter describing this:

Suddenly we saw galloping horses and munitions carts and field guns coming towards us in clouds of dust. A Major who was near me said, 'There's a French battery coming out of action and look, there's another. We thought it time to move towards our own batallion and now everybody seemed overcome by panic and I got a good idea what a rout would be like. I stopped some of the Frenchmen running past but could not get much out of them, except that they were overcome with poison gas which the Germans had let loose. Our batallion then had orders to assist in an attack to regain lost ground. Terrific shelling and firing then took place and the wounded poured in. I should think I was working till midnight without pausing for a moment. Yesterday I saw one of our officers. He says the losses are appalling and nothing was really achieved – it was pure murder. The troops were ordered to advance over open ground in broad daylight against men in entrenched positions and that carnage was the inevitable result.

I am surprised on re-reading some of these letters that they escaped the censor, for they are outspoken on the tragic stupidity of the High Command. My brother, as medical officer, was not exposed to the worst dangers but, as he said, he was extremely lucky to come out of the battle of Ypres alive. Every one of the officers with whom he crossed to France was killed. Eventually he was sent to a base hospital suffering from enteric fever, and afterwards to our great relief he was retained for duty there and did not return to the Front.

In the autumn of 1915 I began to keep a War Diary at school. We were encouraged to do this with an inevitable House Competition in view. Laboriously I drew maps and collected cuttings from the papers to embellish this diary. On the front page is written: 'All the Fronts are taken one after the other in order day by day. The Fronts are underlined in different colours to make clear which is which.' A key to the colouring follows. I think I found this classification reassuring and I am sure I enjoyed it, just as people enjoyed moving little flags tiny distances to and fro on those terrible lines across huge maps. I earned quite a lot of marks for the House with my diary. It was almost as good as shooting a goal in a House match. It contains few personal comments and might have been much more interesting, but by now it has become something of an historical document.

On re-reading it one's impression is of the wool that was continually pulled over our eyes, especially during the first two years. Eastern Front (underlined in blue): 'The Tsar has been visiting the troops in the S.E. where the Germans have been repelled with great losses.' Western Front (underlined in red): 'Sir John French reports in detail the repulse of the German attack, the fire of our artillery and machine guns *completely* stopped this'. And so on and so on.

But all the same no-one talked now of the war being over soon. In November I entered under 'Home Affairs', 'Lord Derby issues an emphatic notice that the 30th of this month is fixed for the last date for young unmarried men to enlist. After that compulsion will be used.' The posters of Lord Kitchener pointing his finger and threatening 'Your King and your country need you' had obviously not been sufficiently effective, nor had the white feathers presented by some ladies to all those men they considered should be in uniform.

At the end of that term, we sang carols: 'Love and joy come to you'. 'Precious little love and joy there'll be about this year,' muttered someone in my ear. There was certainly not much left of the Rupert Brooksian glamour amongst us by then, yet in the summer of 1916 I entered in the diary 'the glorious naval victory at Jutland'. I pasted a large portrait of Sir David Beatty on the opposite page and wrote underneath 'Surely he was, on this famous 21st May, the spirit of England incarnate'. I was also profoundly moved by the drowning of Lord Kitchener, quite unconscious that this was by no means the national tragedy we all thought it.

Zeppelin raids are chronicled, but without much comment, except for the one that occasioned our single alarm at school. Though it was the palest shadow of what I was to experience in the forties, a first-hand account in a letter home is not perhaps without interest:

Feb 1916
Dearest Mummy and Dad
    I really have got something to tell you in this letter. Rumours had been going round that the Zepps were making for Oxford and Windsor. On Thursday we went

to bed and just after the curtains were drawn the factory
siren began to go off frightfully loudly. It is a horribly
weird noise and it went on so long that I thought
something was up – then the lights began very gradually
to go out and I knew then it was Zepps. Then Miss
Logan came in and her voice sounded awfully anxious
and she said, 'I am very afraid it is a Zeppelin, get on
your stockings, shoes, dressing gowns and knickers and
go down to the house study as quickly as possible.' I still
had nearly all the required clothes on so I was the first to
grope my way down for it was pitch dark now. That
horrid noise was still going on and I felt frightened and
the person behind me was just as frightened but when the
noise stopped I felt all right. We all crowded round the
fire talking in subdued whispers and every now and then
there was a horrid silence when we listened for the Zepp.
Miss L read out our names to see if we were all there and
we weren't, for sundry people had gone to bed early and
never woken up, some were in their baths when the lights
went out and had to get out all wet and couldn't find
their clothes and one poor wretch was in the sick room
and was fetched out wrapped in blankets. We were told
to come away from the windows and get near the two
doors as it might be necessary to take us out of doors,
which made it seem frightfully realistic. We had our
school cloaks given us and lay down on the floor to wait.
Then a message came from the police that the Zepps had
lost their way and so they might or might not be near us.
We then had biscuits handed round and Miss L sat in her
dressing gown with her hair hanging all loose and read
Dickens to us by the light of a tiny flashlight. After some
time news came through that the Zepps were nowhere
near us and we heard trains running again so we went
back to bed but were told to have shoes and cloaks ready.
Breakfast wasn't till 9 o'clock!! Miss L stayed up all
night, poor Miss L, she hasn't been feeling well and had
gone to bed early to get extra rest. She seemed awfully

nervous for us. The chief remark made afterwards was
'Well now for *once* we shall have something to write
home about'. One of the maids had hysterics and the
cook comforted her with the advice that we all had to die
someday and she had better make herself ready. The
Zepps had been over Aylesbury about 8 miles away but
there are many rumours as to where they were. However,
it was exciting while it lasted. I have no time to read this
through.

I have preserved a curious newspaper cutting from the old
Westminster Gazette. It is headed 'News for London from the
Hamburger Freunderblett of Saturday last' and is an account
of a reputedly devasting Zeppelin raid in which 'Trafalgar
Square is seriously damaged, the people forced to hide in
cellars and the Underground' and describing 'the inky darkness lit up by searchlights, hospitals filled to overflowing with
the injured, grave destruction of the docks and streets rendered
impassable.' I wrote underneath this cutting: 'Extraordinary
account of a raid in which the Zepps did not come near
London at all and in which all the damage done was that some
horses were killed in Norfolk.' That this fantasy was in fact
prophetic, that indeed it was a pretty accurate description of a
state of affairs that was to be only too actual and too common
thirty years later, all this of course was fortunately hidden from
me.

I do not remember being at all frightened by the Zeppelin
raids or that we took them very seriously. My parents were
moving house in 1917 and we were in a temporary rented
furnished flat in Westminster and my father had to restrain my
mother from rushing out on to the balcony to watch whenever
there was a raid. As a contrast, we had an Irish maid at that
time who used to drop on to her knees and feverishly recite
Ave Maria all the while a raid was on.

The really threatening menace was not from the air but, in
spite of Jutland, from the sea. The submarine war grew in
intensity and food shortages began to be noted in the diary

under the heading of 'Home Affairs'. Meals at school became very dreary, consisting chiefly of potato under various guises. Food rationing was belated and far less efficient than in the Second World War. 'It is left to people's honour to keep to their rations. If they do there will be no need for tickets,' proclaimed Lord Devonport, the first food controller. But honour is a tricky business, as Falstaff knew: Lord Rhonda took over from Lord Devonport and tickets had to be issued for meat and sugar. I transcribed in my diary a poem from Punch:

> I wonder have I dined today?
> My inner man would tell me no.
> And yet an hour or so ago
> I had a dinner bill to pay,
> Yes, I recall the witty play
> Of talk – the table white as snow.
> I wonder have I dined today? My inner man would tell
>   me no,
> Only a barmaid perhaps could say
> How much to fancy's aid I owe.
> Enough – Lord Rhonda wills it so
> But still my doubt will not away
> I wonder, have I dined today?

The Russian Revolution is chronicled from day to day, at first in glowing excitement but becoming apprehensive as it grew clear that the new regime meant the total collapse of the Eastern Front. In spite of America's long-awaited declaration of war, things were looking pretty black throughout 1917. I recorded without comment the peace moves made by Mr Henderson and the Labour Party, and their abortive efforts to attend an International Socialist conference at Stockholm to meet German socialists. I had by this time left school, but continued my War Diary until early in 1918, the last entry being a depressing one on 'the serious decline of our shipping owing to enemy action'.

But my parents were always invincibly optimistic, upheld by
their faith, and, once my brother was out of the firing line, I
don't think I suffered any real fear or hardship. Certainly the
1914–18 war made no impact on me comparable to what I
experienced in the Second World War. I was extremely lucky
in that I lost no-one near and dear to me, though the unending
daily casualty lists were terrible. But what I chiefly remember
feeling throughout all but the first months is the menace of a
dark cloud that was apt to invade joy. For instance, the winter
of 1916–17 was long and very cold. One day in the holidays I
had been skating and a glorious time I had had of it, but
running home along the crisp, white, empty roads under the
stars, suddenly my exhilaration faded and died at the thought
of the soldiers in their bitter trenches.

In spite of the war I was happy on the whole during my final
school year. It was still boring to spend most of my leisure
playing lacrosse, but I had reached a respectable position in the
second House team and, as for cricket, my Better Half had the
brilliant idea of getting our respective parents to object to our
playing in our spectacles (made then of glass). We were no use
without them, and so we were excused games and allowed to
garden instead.

The garden plots beyond the lake were assiduously cultivated because, curiously enough, the only school prizes
allowed were for the best gardens. Each plot was shared
between a senior and a junior. I had served my apprenticeship
the summer before and now had an underling. I wrote a House
Alphabet at the time which immortalized her:

A is for Annis who gardens with me,
An amiable child and as quiet as can be.

The amiable child grew up to be a famous doctor – Dame
Annis Gillie. We carried off the first prize for gardens in
triumph, owing chiefly to her efforts. Our delphiniums were
especially noteworthy. Sometimes in cricket hours, when not
gardening, I was able to commandeer the one little canoe and

slip away to the furthest corner of the lake where, among the tall secretive rushes, I could read and dream in peace.

That year, too, work became increasingly interesting. I was now specializing in English and History for a long-extinct examination called the Higher Local, designed originally to provide post-school qualification before any university was open to girls. Although it was gradually becoming less unusual to aim at further education, and though London had actually granted degrees to women, this exam still lingered on and was taken more for interest's sake than with any particular aim in view.

There were only two of us doing English and three in the History class, which was the more interesting for one of us was a Catholic, one a Unitarian, and one, myself, a Presbyterian. Our teacher was Anglican and we were doing the 17th century religious Wars, so discussion was animated and broadening. The Sixth Form were privileged to work in the Library, which was a gracious room with its big gothic windows, polished oak floor, stout little oak tables, and an intriguing period door simulating rows of leatherbound folio volumes. This was the first of a number of libraries in which I have worked. I have loved them all and in each have experienced a blessed fusion of exhilaration and peace.

I was made a prefect during my last year, which brought further privileges. For instance, prefects did not have their strayed property confiscated. The penalty for two of these confiscations in a week was to lose one's ration of sweets and, for each subsequent article, a buttonhole had to be worked on a strip of material before our 7.30 breakfast. The week I was made prefect I had no fewer than six buttonholes against my name. I was in despair, I hated working buttonholes, and, even more, I hated having to get up early. Then I was suddenly told I was to be a prefect. It was unbelievably opportune.

In the Sixth Form we got to know the staff as human beings. The Archangel took us for Scripture when she had the time. I remember an essay: 'It is one of the great tragedies of history that Constantine and not Marcus Aurelius was the first

84

Christian Emperor'. She used to throw subjects like that at us out of the blue. But not only did she now teach us; she also invited us, four at a time, to dine with her. We dined in state in her own room, wearing our best white dresses, and she too wore evening dress and treated us with courtesy.

I admired her very much, but I did not fall in love with her. That delicious experience was reserved for my English and History mistresses – both at once. My English mistress was a cheerful, round-faced person with prominent hazel eyes and copper-coloured hair. She had a lively sense of humour and she gave me a lifelong appreciation of Chaucer and of Pope. I adored her and she liked being adored. I presented her with yellow roses from my garden and she wore a spray the next morning pinned to her dress and winked at me.

The History mistress always reminded me of Napoleon. She strutted about the platform, darting sideways glances at the class from her very bright black eyes. She was formidable – you could not have given *her* roses. She was very restless and had a habit of clipping and unclipping the press-buttons on the side of her skirt as she strode up and down. She could be sarcastic but never cruelly so. Before our exam she gave each of us a piece of advice. When she came to me she said: 'You'll be all right if you don't stop to try and solve the problems of the universe in the middle of your paper.' I was at the same time perplexed, annoyed, and gratified by this remark. 'What made her say this? Of course I wouldn't be so silly! But anyway she had said I would be all right. She must have been a good teacher for in her time she inspired no fewer than six of us in different years to read History at her own old college, Lady Margaret Hall at Oxford. Alas, she left to do war work before my Sixth Form year was up. Her successor was dreadfully conscientious and hardworking, copying out pages and pages of notes which we were supposed to digest and regurgitate in due course in our essays. This was no substitute for our old stirring discussions.

Worshipping my two divinities made me work harder than I would otherwise have done and gilded all my days. It was a beneficial and gentle way to encounter romance, and of course it was the fashion. Even my sensible down to earth Better Half had to pretend to fall in love with some member of the staff, though she was a poor hand at it and kept forgetting which one it was. On the whole it was a harmless and natural state of affairs, and much less upsetting than boyfriends.

It probably won't be believed, but it is nonetheless true that we never talked of boys or even mentioned sex, and I don't think we were troubled by this. Few of us, indeed, knew anything much about sex, for it was before Freud had made any general impression, before too, the veils of prudery which had enwrapped our mothers had been altogether dispersed. We lucky ones breathed a freer air than they, freer too than our grandchildren, bombarded as they are by all branches of the omnipresent media. Pressure-free in our protracted childhood, we were let alone. Of course some of us were more ignorant and incurious than others. I myself was both, to a marked degree. All births were virgin births to me and fortuitous besides. I longed at one time for a baby sister or brother. Almost every day I used to come home from the High School expectantly. 'Perhaps a baby has come,' I would say to myself, 'Perhaps it has happened today. I'll go in very quietly and then they will tell me or perhaps I shall hear it crying.' But I never did and one day I suppose I gave up hoping.

The miracle of new life was first revealed to me by my rabbits. I had noticed the doe becoming very fat and William, the gardener, had told me that she was carrying babies inside her and that he would make me a separate hutch for the buck as father rabbits did not like their children. This seemed to me immensely exciting and extraordinary. William showed me the nest the doe was making in her bedroom. 'You leave her alone in there,' he said, 'and she'll bring them out and show them to you when they're ready for it.' I did as I was told and was rewarded by the astonishing fact that one day I found I had eight rabbits instead of two, but I was no nearer knowing how this had occurred.

I never asked questions of anyone, least of all my mother.

Instinctively I knew she would have been deeply embarrassed. Like most middle class girls of her generation, she had been brought up on complete ignorance. She had not even understood what was happening when her first child was well on the way, and had thought herself ill until enlightened by a friend. Her ingrained prudery was lifelong; when sunbathing first came into fashion she confessed, half-laughing, her horror – 'all these bodies!' On the eve of my wedding day she said to me nervously, 'I expect you know what you ought to know already, don't you?' and was obviously relieved when I said that I did. However, though she did not teach me anything about sex, she did teach me much about married love. I grew up taking it for granted that this must be rooted and grounded in mutual trust and equal partnership. After the rabbits, my sex education was at a standstill until that first gloomy holiday of the war at Nairn when my sister, probably to relieve boredom, suddenly took it upon herself to enlighten me as to the facts of life, which she managed to do very unconvincingly as I simply did not believe her. It seemed too preposterous and, when I read *Adam Bede* soon after, I was completely mystified as to what had really happened in the summerhouse between Arthur and Hetty. The Bible didn't help either with its vague talk of 'knowing' people and 'lying' with them; in fact it worried me quite a lot on one occasion, after I had had a picnic with my cousin on the Downs lying on the grass close beside me, and he had kissed me. Would that be enough to start a baby? According to the Bible, it would. However, I soon got over that anxiety, for the most part I was not bothered. I felt quite confident that I should marry some day and have a large family. I had fixed on one of my brother's nicest friends and was sad and a little affronted when it appeared that he was not content to wait for me to grow up, and had actually got engaged to someone else. But there was somebody waiting for me, I was sure, and meanwhile I was too absorbed in my school divinities and in the campaigns of Louis XIV to pay attention to sex.

I owe my Oxford career to the great Duke of Marlborough.

I had happened on a good biography of him in the holidays before my Higher Local exam and was lucky enough to get a question in the English History paper on an estimation of his character. I enjoyed myself on that one, and I am sure that it was this that got me the Distinction which in those days secured a place at college. I had not thought of the university before, but now I was fired with ambition. Oxford and Lady Margaret Hall was the inevitable choice, as that was the college of my History mistress, and our latest head girl had proceeded thither with a scholarship. However, I had first to pass Responsions ('Smalls'), an exam consisting of a fairly stiff Latin and Greek section and a fairly easy Maths paper. I had never learnt a word of either Latin or Greek and was exceedingly bad at Maths which I had dropped anyway a year before. 'Do you think if one wants a thing badly enough one can get it?' I enquired of the Archangel. 'Not always,' she replied, kindly but firmly, 'though it is good to try.'

So once more, when it had been settled that I was leaving school, I came back again. This time, my place had been filled and I was to be boarded out for one term to start on my uncongenial studies. A girl from another House and I were to live with the doctor and his wife, who had a comfortable, pretty old house in the High Street. I did not know this other girl well and I can't remember now why she was there, or what she was doing, but she was a merry sort of clown and we got on pleasantly together.

It was at the very start of this new phase of school life that something happened that greatly troubled and shook me. A girl called Nora who had not been at school very long had become very attached to Grace and myself. She was junior to us, and perhaps we had been kind to her when she first arrived on the scene, for she certainly repaid us in many small ways. She was a gentle, loving person, very fond of her mother and baby brother, and often homesick. Two days after the beginning of term, she was taken ill with what proved to be meningitis and she died that same week.

She was supposed to have caught the disease from a soldiers' camp near her home, and the whole House was immediately isolated from the rest of the school. As I had travelled from London in the school train sitting next to Nora, I was included in the quarantine and moved from my new quarters in the town back into the House, where a bed was put up for me in the Matron's sitting-room. I was grateful for this, needing to be with Grace, and glad of the occupation which I shared with the prefects of helping the juniors with their work, as the staff were not allowed to come and give us lessons.

But my father had taken fright, and he was always a man of action. Suddenly I was informed that a taxi was at the door to take me to a nursing home in Reading to be under the observation of an unknown doctor whom my father had heard was a specialist in brain diseases. He was to watch me for symptoms. Miserable but helpless, and still, of course, suffering from the shock of Nora's death, I was bundled into the taxi with my night things hastily collected by the matron. I had never taken such a long journey by car before – 20 or 30 miles. The only book I had caught up to take with me was Thackeray's *Four Georges*, and this was my sole and not particularly entrancing source of entertainment at the bleak nursing home, where I was immediately put to bed. The fact that I had started a heavy head cold did not help matters – it might be a symptom!

After a day or two, however, it became obvious that my cold was disappearing and almost certain that I was not sickening for meningitis. My father would not allow my mother to come to see me, nor did he come himself, and the telephone was not used for conversations at a distance in those days, so I felt very lonely and miserable. But things improved – the doctor was kind and, I think, sorry for me, and took me out on his rounds with him. A car ride was still a rare treat – it was an open one, of course – and I did not at all mind sitting in it waiting while he made his calls. I took *The Four Georges* with me but for the most part I just sat and looked at the landscape. He had several patients in the villages, and the country round Reading was then unspoiled. (I did not know the meaning of 'spoiled' and 'unspoiled' country till years after.) I found the glimpses of the smoothly flowing Thames, the warm red old Berkshire houses, the little churches, the great domed yellowing chestnut and beech trees, all basking in the autumn sun, soothing to my unquiet spirit. A middle-aged, wounded Canadian officer shared these trips. He was fatherly and courteous to the solitary, dispossessed schoolgirl whom he couldn't account for, and discussed gravely with me the intricacies of English education.

I thought much about Nora. She was the first friend of my own age that I had lost. I was not troubled for her. I knew that she was good enough to go straight to the Heaven I did not question, but I could not bear to think I should never see her again and I was very sad for her mother, from whom Grace and I had had a heartbroken letter. I was very glad when I was allowed to go back to school and deeply ashamed that my father had made such a fuss.

I enjoyed beginning Latin and Greek, especially the latter, which seemed to me very romantic and special. For Maths I had individual coaching. 'I cannot understand how it is that you are able to tackle Euclid quite well and are so hopelessly stupid over your arithmetic.' Neither did I, but I hoped the Euclid would pull me through. Luckily, I was not required to do algebra.

I liked lodging at Dr Huggins' house. He was a quiet little man whom we scarcely ever saw, and his wife was a dear. She was Irish, plump and dark, a very good cook, and had second-sight and a stock of marvellous ghost stories.

We spent most of our time at school, but on Sundays we much enjoyed the freedom and homeliness of that comfortable Georgian house, with its view of the wide, interesting High Street. Mrs Huggins gave us a splendid Sunday dinner in spite of the war, or perhaps it seemed so splendid because we compared it with the school meals, and afterwards we sat, somnolent and content, in her upstairs sitting room before a huge fire while she recounted incidents of her own visionary powers. So the term slipped away, and that Christmas I really did leave school, as it was settled that I should continue to coach for Responsions privately at home.

My parents were wholehearted in their support, my father thinking the education of daughters as important as that of sons, a point of view most unusual in fathers at that time. But they were unfortunate in their first choice of a coach for me. He was the scholarly elderly husband of my mother's suffragette friend. I don't think they were well off, and she arranged this as she arranged everything else in their lives. He was, I believe, a good classical scholar, but he was not a good teacher. He was content to take me ambling gently though my Caesar and Xenophon with the help of a crib, and it was not until it was too late that it was discovered that I had to cope with grammar papers and a Latin prose – the latter designed for schoolboys who had learned Latin from babyhood.

I went up to Oxford to sit for the examination (in which, of course, I failed) and stayed with my parents at a guesthouse in Norham Road. I thought North Oxford was hideous and continued to think so for many years, until the charm of its stained-glass windows and dusky beeches and laburnums and lilacs and pink may trees gradually grew dear to me. But, of course, I fell in love with Oxford proper and was more than ever determined to get there. I was not downcast by this first failure, in fact I didn't expect anything else, and was quite pleased I had passed in my set books. There were plenty more chances in the year ahead and, as it turned out, I needed them!

My next coach was a rather horrid little man at a Tutorial Institution in Red Lion Square. We sat together at a table in an empty fusty classroom, and he sat very close and put an arm round my shoulders to point out phrases in my book. I edged away from him and was always glad to get out into the open air again to walk up the narrow street into Holborn and into the ABC shop at the corner to have my lunch. My mother favoured the old Aereated Bread Company shops rather than the Lyons ones that were springing up everywhere, though they were very similar, quite small and dark and unpretentious. To me they seemed worldly and fine. I would have a slice of veal and ham pie, a bun, a glass of ginger beer for a shilling and sixpence. I always spent just that sum and then I would take the tube to Charing Cross and go home.

I felt very grown-up travelling alone on these weekly journeys. I had put up my hair while still at school, a significant and serious affair, which most of us felt was only right and proper in the Sixth Form. A circle of friends usually attended and assisted at the first venture. Hairpins and advice were in plentiful supply. It was a complicated process of coils and partings and rolls, resulting in an unfamiliar weight on one's head and a cold feeling at the back of one's neck. It took a lot of time, but it was worth it for the respect and admiration that it commanded.

Hair up, skirts longer and tighter (hobble skirts almost impossible to walk in were the fashion then), journeys to London by myself and, at home, homesick soldiers to entertain. Two especially I remember who used to come frequently to tea. One, very young, who asked me to play a Mozart Sonata to him over and over again, and another who enjoyed a game of billiards. I flirted a little, very innocently, with them but they were too nice and too unhappy to take advantage of me. Both were killed almost immediately after reaching the Front.

This was the last summer we spent at Oakhampstead. My father was retiring and had bought a little farmhouse in the Sussex downlands, of which more hereafter. It was a memorable summer because of this, and because my elder sister came to us to have her first baby. I seem to have had an unfortunate habit of having the wrong book at the wrong moment: when homesick I read *Villette*, when at the Reading Nursing Home in great need of cheerful entertainment I read *The Four Georges*, and when waiting for the baby to arrive I found myself horrorstruck at the account of Kitty Levin's ordeal in *War and Peace*. I lay awake in my attic bedroom on the fateful night listening for cries and shrieks, but I heard nothing but the opening and shutting of doors and in the morning I was told that my niece had arrived without much trouble and was allowed to see her.

This was better than any number of rabbits and extraordinarily moving and exciting – a new person in the family, almost as good as the baby sister or brother I had always longed for. All babies in those days, unless there were abnormal circumstances, were born at home with a monthly nurse and the family doctor in attendance, and the husband made himself scarce. My brother-in-law and I were packed off for the day with sandwiches and told not to come back till evening. We had a wonderful walk through the pine woods talking endlessly about the baby's golden future.

In the autumn I had another go at Responsions. This time I stayed in Hall; I slept in a room belonging to a History student and I surveyed her books and her belongings with envy and awe. The room looked out on the gardens and the river, a 'charmed magic casement' it appeared to me, and I swore to myself that I would one day have a similar enchanted room of my own. However, I failed to pass in my Latin prose and in Maths, and this time I *was* a little depressed. But there was much to divert me, for when I went home, it was not to Oakhampstead and the town I had known from babyhood, but to the Sussex farmhouse that I had never before seen. I had felt sad and resentful at leaving the old house and the garden with the oak tree and the elm meadow. 'I shall never love another home so well,' I thought, but I was quite mistaken.

The taxi that I had taken at Eastbourne station climbed Beachy Head. It was a misty, autumn evening with a smouldering sun just disappearing into the sea. We turned inland and came down among soft layers of Downs, the car shuffling through the rich, thick dust of the narrow white road and drawing up beside a farm track that led up a slope between stubble fields.

'I can't take her up here, it's too rough,' said my driver. 'But I'll carry up your bag, Miss.' I thanked him and followed, stumbling in the gathering darkness and sniffing at the cold freshness of the air. There was a tall, evergreen hedge and the crouching shapes of two old sycamores and, beyond, the little one-eyed grey house. Then we were at the door which was flung open and I stepped into my new home. It was full of glowing life in firelight and candlelight and red dahlias on the table and welcoming words and all the bustle of a meal in preparation and, outside the uncurtained window, no lights at all and no movement and no sound, only the enfolding dark hills.

My bedroom was at the back of the house. Everything in it was nicer than in my old one, for now I had inherited the furniture that had been my married sister's and, besides, there was a little writing-desk in one corner and over the fireplace, instead of the tiresome child and her dolls saying their prayers, there was one of my uncle's watercolours which I had always admired. I was enchanted. I slept soundly that night in my sister's much more comfortable bed, and woke to look eagerly out of my low window. The view was free and open, without a single building or tree to break up its sweeping outline, bold against the sky. I jumped from my bed and opened the casement wide, put my head out, and caught the murmur of the sea. But almost at once this was drowned by the sound of water being pumped up in the yard and my father's voice calling me to breakfast.

The house was not much more than a cottage: it was about 100 years old and had once been the home of a learned shepherd who was interested in archaeology and geology, and had known Thomas Huxley. It had its own little farmyard with brick and flint cattle troughs, and a small barn roofed with golden lichen-covered tiles. There was no water supply, other than rain water, no bathroom, outdoor sanitation, no electric light or gas! The nearest building was the old lighthouse and the nearest shop two or so miles away in the village. In those practically car-free days, it was indeed remote. All these inconveniences added to its charm in my eyes – lamps, candles, pump, and the earth closet among the bushes and the birds. The house itself, though not beautiful, was so neat and compact and assured, sitting there on the slope of the combe with an incomparable view on every side.

I was completely won over from the very first. I did not forget my old home, but I ceased to mourn it. That month held the transient joy of a sort of camping holiday for us all, for we were only to stay till the November mists and shorter days should drive us to London, where my father had taken a furnished flat for the winter months. We were not really to settle in till next spring. My mother, of course, was not without a domestic help, and one that took all the drawbacks of the place in her stride. I do not know how my mother heard of Mrs Hitchins – probably just through a local agency. She was a small, sandy-haired woman with a fierce, pointed little face like a fox, but she was very amiable and a good cook. That she was always called Mrs Hitchins and never by her Christian name was significant, and though she wore a plain white apron over her dress, you could not call it uniform. In fact there was not longer 'a baize door'. I used to like to sit by the kitchen fire and chat to Mrs Hitchins, but it never occurred to me to lift a finger there. It was a cheerful, light little kitchen and opened straight on to the Downs where, even so late in the year, larks always seemed to be singing.

At Oakhampstead the tradesmen called every day for orders and delivery, but at Hodcombe no one called but the postwoman who was a very wirey, weatherbeaten person, which was not surprising, as she had to walk a wide round in all weathers over the Downs to outlying farms and cottages as well as to the village. She delivered and collected mail in one visit, arriving punctually before our breakfast each morning. We had to have the outgoing letters all ready, for she did not like to be kept waiting. The post, though reaching us in this primitive fashion, was unbelievably quick and reliable. It was possibly to send a letter to London one morning and get an answer the following one – and all for one penny.

I was sorry when our candlelit evenings got longer and the time came to pack up and leave the country. But we would be back again in March and meanwhile it was interesting to be going to live in London and not merely to visit it. I had got over my childhood fear of the place and looked forward to exploring it. Our flat, comfortable but ordinary after Hodcombe, was in Westminster, a good centre for exploration.

The London of seventy years ago only exists now in pockets. Even the Abbey and the Houses of Parliament, Hyde Park Corner and Buckingham Palace, all within easy reach of the flat, are different, dwarfed as they now appear by high-rise buildings, seen only amid a roaring sea of traffic. I used often to wander about the streets by myself; there was always a friendly 'Bobby' on duty somewhere near in case I lost my way. There might be a Zeppelin raid (though I was never caught up in one), but there was certainly no mugging. Also, many of the sights which had distressed me as a child seemed to have vanished. There were no more barefooted children or crossing sweepers, and no more poor cab or bus horses.

A favourite walk was down Buckingham Gate past its sedate, small Queen Anne houses and the Wellington Barracks where the Guards lived, or what was left of them. Then into St James's Park from where the skyline of distant buildings looked like an 'insubstantial pageant', past the statue of Queen Victoria, for whom I had once prayed, on through the House Guards, down Whitehall, and so at last to the Abbey.

The Cloisters were a good place in which to revise my Latin texts. Perhaps thoughts of the studious monks who used to work there would inspire me. I would sit myself down in one of the worn stone recesses and open my books, and often I would have the place to myself for most of the morning. Sometimes I would take a bus to the City and prowl round St Pauls, but I never liked the Cathedral so much as the Abbey, though the little Dickensian streets nearby and the flavour of the City attracted me.

At Christmas my brother had leave. The shops did their wartime best and we went shopping together. Our 'village shop' was the Army & Navy Stores, conveniently near, solid, spacious, and quiet. Regent Street was more alluring and beautiful, the lower part of Nash's gracious facade still intact. Walking in the streets was pleasant for they never seemed crowded, but if we wanted more space there were the Parks. It was possible to walk continuously through these from St James's to Kensington Gardens. One day when we did this, the snow was thick and unsullied for wide stretches and the great royal trees were weighted down with it. There were skaters shouting to each other on the Round Pond, making the distant hum of the city outside the gates sound like winter bees On the way home there were purple and green shadows on the snow and the sun burned on the horizon like the flaming Zeppelin I had seen over Hampstead.

For the war dragged on. The end was not yet in sight and as soon as Christmas was over my brother had to return to his Army hospital and I got down to my grind for Responsions again. I was doing my Greek and Maths by correspondence courses then, but I had Latin coaching at home. I can remember nothing at all about this particular coach, except the fact that I thought him efficient and encouraging, and I was fairly confident of having passed when I sat for the exam for the third time in the spring. However, in due course, the fateful telegram arrived from Oxford with the usual dismal 'Failed' inscribed within. I wrote for particulars and received a note from the Principal of Lady Margaret Hall:

Dear Miss Yeo,
You have failed to satisfy the Examiners in all your
    subjects without exception.
Yours sincerely,
Henrietta Jex Blake.

The tautology of this brief note seemed heartless and crude, and the situation was serious for I knew that the Hall would not keep my place open for me indefinitely. I could sit for the wretched bugbear of an exam again in the summer, but that would probably be my last chance. People tried to comfort me. 'It wasn't *your* fault. They don't read the papers for 'Smalls', you know. They just throw them up in the air and the ones that come down the right way up they pass.' And, 'Did you know that Mr Gladstone failed seven times?' But how was I to make sure that my papers came down right side up, and I didn't really believe it about Mr. Gladstone. Besides I couldn't afford to fail as often as that. I think my mother worried about me and wanted me to give up, but I swore to myself that next time I would make it.

It was lovely to be in Sussex again. At Hodcombe the Downs were covered with cowslips and the larks were singing like mad. My father was full of plans for digging a front and back garden out of the chalk so that he could grow his beloved roses and my mother have her herbaceous borders, for these would need protection from the wind. At present there was just the two ancient, gnarled sycamores and a vegetable patch. Eventually he achieved this and invented a unique family golf/croquet course which went down a steep slope, round the herbaceous plot up the hill again, through the Euonymus hedge, and ended on the only level stretch between the trees. Everyone who visited us had to play this game. My father was also intending to add a bathroom, indoor sanitation, and an extra bedroom, but this was not to be started on that year and, for the present, we were still to lead the simple life.

I continued my correspondence courses in Maths and Greek, but for Latin I now had the luck to hit upon a really good teacher. He was a master at one of the many prep schools in Eastbourne, and was interesting, very clear, and also experienced. Twice a week I set out to walk over the Downs to his house in Meads, the scholastic and highly respectable west end of the town. There was a choice of two routes. One climbed the steep slope behind Hodcombe to the old dew pond and continued, on the top of the world, steering a course between two hill farms until it crossed the road that led out to Beachy Head. From there a little gorse-enclosed track led down steeply to the red-brick paths and tree-lined streets of civilization. The other way was more sheltered. It took me first across arable land and then up a gently rising combe which always seemed particularly remote and peaceful, though as a matter of fact I hardly ever met anyone on either route.

Sometimes my mother would meet me halfway on the way home. There was a cattle trough at our meeting-place with a flat stone beside it, under which she might leave a message, generally in rhyme, if she could not come. I enjoyed these solitary journeys. Occasionally it was rough weather, but I did not mind rain or wind. What was a bit frightening were the blank, white sea mists which could descend quite suddenly and blot out everything so that I had to guess my direction blindly step by step. But as spring turned into summer, my whole way was scented with thyme and the spicy, coconut smell of flowering gorse.

There was never any noise, no sounds at all but the wind, the sheep's bells, the seagulls, and the larks. During my lifetime so many sounds have disappeared or been drowned by the ever-present machines of all kinds – on roads, in the air, in the fields, on the water, and even in the house. (A neighbour of mine who was temporarily without radio and television was asked lately by a pitying child: 'What *do* you do for noise?') But once, as common 'background music', one heard the crowing and clucking of cocks and hens, the clop-clopping of horses, the sounds of cuckoos, nightingales and rooks, and in towns street cries: 'chairs to mend', 'knives to grind', and the bell of the muffin man. All these have gone or become rare, and the little noiseless noises that remain forever, the gentle winds blowing through grass and leaves, flowing water, distant church bells, and the small birds' cries have to be listened for at all too short intervals and rescued from the din of this clamourous age.

That July I packed my bag and once more made for Oxford. This time I had a large, empty room looking out on the bicycle sheds. The late owner had obviously just gone down and had taken all her belongings with her, so that there were no books to distract me. I slept very badly because it was important to sleep well, and the next morning my head ached and it was the Latin prose day. It was the worst one yet, all about the Gunpowder Plot, quoting the very letter that Francis Tresham sent to Lord Monteagle to warn him. The lovely fan vaulting of the Divinity Schools where we sat for the exam seemed a symbol of all I aspired to. I gazed up at it. How on earth to translate 'gunpowder' into Latin? Was the wretched Sir Francis to rob me of my hopes? I was very much afraid he was. The rest of the papers were not bad, but I was quite certain I had failed once again, and this time fatally. 'Oh, never mind,' said my mother. 'There are other things in the world.' But I minded very much, and when the orange telegram was handed in by the telegraph boy, I was afraid to open it.

My aunt did it for me, as my parents were gone shopping in Eastbourne. She glanced at it and then waved it above her head in triumph. I snatched it from her. There was my passport to felicity. 'Passed: Bellaby'. (Bellaby, Clerk to the University Schools, a sanctified name for evermore!) I couldn't wait to tell my parents. 'I'll go in and find them,' I said. 'If I hurry I'll catch them at lunch, they'll be sure to be at Boots' Restaurant.' This was our favourite lunching place and sure enough they were still there, for I had sped over the Downs on wings of exaltation. My father took me into the nearest jewellers and bought me a brooch to mark the occasion. Of course I was pleased at this, but needed no brooch to make me happy. My cup of joy was already quite full.

Now the rest of the summer spread itself before me, inviting me to spend its spacious days as I liked. True, I had a reading list of history books sent me from Oxford, but after my uncongenial struggles with language and maths, they would be only part of the pleasure of life in general. Bryce's *Holy Roman Empire*, lazily perused in the sunshine, sitting on the old barn steps, retains for me throughout life an air of cheerful serenity, quite at variance with its contents. No longer having to trek regularly to Eastbourne, I was free to explore the country in other directions. The way to the village lay along bridle paths and passed only two buildings – the cottage from which we daily fetched our milk and the big farm that had once been the manor house and which lay in a fold of the hills about half a mile from the church. Beyond the church was the village green around which clustered the Tiger Inn, the school, the forge, and the shop.

This was the least inviting and nastiest village shop I have ever known. Empty, or almost empty, cardboard boxes were piled precariously everywhere – sweet jars, jostled rolls of material, oranges, and decaying bananas sat upon post cards and telegraph forms. It seemed a marvel when, after a long search, the required goods were at last produced. It was kept by a worried little man and his pale, silent daughter, Elsie. Elsie was the unlikely love of a middle-aged farmer at the Manor Farm. They were to be seen silently walking together on summer evenings or, when it rained, sitting staring into space in the shelter of a farm shed. His two elderly spinster sisters, who kept house for him, thought Elsie below them and no match for him, and would not let her into the house. I thought this an interesting Hardy-ish sort of situation, but they were a very unromantic couple. I never saw them laughing or talking together, or even holding hands.

Living so much away from the village, as we did, I did not know many of its inhabitants, but before my father had brought Hadcombe we had stayed a short while at the Forge with Luke, the blacksmith, and his wife. The Forge and its adjoining cottage backed straight on to the chalk down and its only view was from the front, where it opened directly on to the road. It had a narrow verandah along its whole length where one could sit and watch the horses coming to be shod and the children going to and fro to school and other interesting, leisurely happenings. Today a ceaseless river of traffic rushes by the place, which has no longer any identity.

The Tiger Inn was colour-washed in an appropriate orange tint and formed part of a pretty group of old cottages facing the Green. Except in unpleasant weather it is nowadays hardly possible to see these buildings, so cluttered up is the little green with cars and coaches, but when I first knew it there was never anyone about but a cluster of children let out of school or the farm labourers dropping into the Inn after their day's work.

Up the hill from the Forge was a second village, only a hamlet really, but possessing its own tiny ancient church, a pond, and, best of all, a windmill. The old miller, Harry, was a friend of mine and used to let me go into the mill. He was to be the last of a long line of millers and this made him sad. There was little for him to do now, but 'When I was a boy the folks used all to come for the grist, I was kept busy enough then.' Still, sometimes I was lucky and the sails would be turning when I climbed the hill. I would hurry to get inside and, entranced, would watch through the window the huge arms, like those of some enormous giant, go sweeping past, and feel a strange excitement as the whole mill vibrated around me. Harry told me that when he was a boy he used to clamber out on to one of the sails and, clinging fast, would be whirled and whirled round in the air. I gasped in admiration and horror. 'Not when the wind was strong and not if my Dad was about,' said Harry.

The Vicar was a quiet, shy man, at least he was shy with my overpowering father, but he was much liked and respected in the village. He was a bachelor but loved children and was loved by them. He taught enthusiastically in the village school and it was his boast that during the ten years he had known it, there had never been any truancy. He and the schoolmaster were great friends. 'I deplore the latest fad in education,' he said, 'that Hadow scheme, taking away all our eleven-year-olds and sending them to the big town school – and by motor bus, too, at our expense. Country children should have a country education and should not be treated as if they were all going into factories.' He was a great lover of the countryside, of its flowers and birds and beasts and its local history, and was the author of three pleasant, informative books on East Sussex.

My father, by now, had forged strong links with St Andrews, the Presbyterian Church in Eastbourne but, though God still talked with a Scotch accent, yet we did sometimes walk over the hills to evensong at the village church. My father's attitude towards Anglicanism was, I thought, always slightly patronizing, but unless it was 'High', he was friendly and cooperative and the Vicar would sometimes ask him to read the lesson. His sermons were much shorter and simpler than those of Dr Reid at St Andrews, but nonetheless sincere. He would drop in now and then for tea and a chat with us. But we did not really mix much with the village – we were too far away and my father did not get a car until some years later. We had very few visitors.

I don't think this troubled my parents at all – they were sufficient unto themselves.

It had been bold of them to dig up their roots and change their way of life so thoroughly, but they were both still very active and they found plenty to do. My mother, feeling the need for something to take the place of all her Temperance and church work, began to learn braille, so as to be able to transcribe books for the blind.

Before tapes or talking books were invented the braille library was of supreme importance, and my mother added to it a good many books of her own choice, both fiction and non-fiction, transcribed during the rest of her active life. But at first she found it hard work. She used to say how good it was for her, hasty and inaccurate by nature, to *have* to take great care, for if she made a mistake at the end of a page, she had to do the whole page again. My father was equally busy with the compiling of a lectionary to be used in the Presbyterian churches.

His and my mother's leisure were spent in gardening, walking, and reading. Neither missed the absence of social life that summer and I did not really miss it either. I was used to being without friends of my own age at home, boarding school having been fatal to local friendships.

However, when my aunt took her annual long visit to the Devon cousins, there was room for other members of the family to come and stay. My cousin Eleanor was one of these. She was my mother's niece and had married Bruce (Barbellion), one of the Devonshire cousins on my father's side, so she was doubly related and besides was special to me as we shared the same birthday. She was indeed a very special sort of person. She had French ancestry from her father which accounted, perhaps, for a certain elegance and gaiety. she was not exactly beautiful, but she had great charm. Her eyes were more green than hazel, wide-set in a pale, faintly freckled face, and she had a habit of opening them very wide when she was interested or amused. She had a peculiarly attractive voice – soft and slightly nasal. She carried herself like a queen.

She knew when she married Bruce (though he did not) that he had sclerosis and would not live long, but she faced this with great courage and nursed him to the end. She married again, a wild irresponsible being, the son of Edwin Abbey, a Victorian artist. He disappeared abroad before their son was born and no-one knew what ultimately became of him. Eleanor supported herself and the children by dressmaking and designing and by interior decorating. She established a theatrical connection and worked sometimes for Oliver Messel. Eleanor widened my horizons and especially quickened my appreciation of the beauty of objects in relation to one another. Although tragedy had already overtaken her, my memory of her on this visit is not at all tragic. I see her on the footpath by the dewpond in a green dress, coming towards me with her springing tread, her hands full of wild flowers. She was a life-enhancer.

Another visitor that summer was my little deaf aunt from Brighton. She was the youngest of her family of five girls and three boys, and had been left stone deaf after measles at three years old. She was my mother's favourite sister and a fairer, smaller edition of her, with the same quick movements and the same sly sense of humour. Her very blue eyes always seemed to have a twinkle in them. You could not be sorry for her. She was very independent: she had looked after her parents in old age until they died, this care falling naturally on her as she was the only unmarried one of the family, and, afterwards, she refused to make her home with any of her sisters or brothers, much though they would have welcomed her. She chose to live alone in Brighton, which she loved. My father tried in vain to get her to move to Eastbourne where she would be nearer us but she did not like Eastbourne – 'too respectable,' she said. He always maintained that she was the ablest of my mother's family and that, had she not been deaf, she would have made her mark. She had learnt to lip-read when she was still very young, and managed to understand most people except men with beards or moustaches. She always had to choose a minister who was clean-shaven and then she could follow the sermon without much difficulty. She loved reading and walking, and never seemed lonely or bored, though she enjoyed a visit to us, I think, flitting very quietly about the house, twinkling, and talking in the softest and clearest of voices.

Next my sister came with her baby. This was a mixed pleasure. I was thrilled with my niece and I was fond of my sister, but was never at ease when she was about. She was rebellious, impatient, and devastatingly outspoken. We had all suffered from her tongue, and naturally my Victorian father did not spare his tongue in return. Lightning and thunder were the result. But it was not his authority only that alienated her. She shrank equally from his Victorian sentimentality. My poor father had only to remark (as it must be confessed he often did) that poppies were his favourite flower because my mother had been wearing a hat with poppies in it when he first saw her, or that the gentle contours of the downs were like a woman's breasts, for my sister to recoil in disgust. Marriage and motherhood had not altered their unquiet relationship and I remember that visit as being particularly uneasy.

My second sister was at home too for a spell. She had been serving as a VAD nurse in the Middle East where she had had a riding accident which deprived her totally of the sense of smell and, for the rest of her life, partially of taste. She never once complained of this.

We three and the baby had climbed one day up the hill to the dew pond. We spread a rug out on the sweet-smelling turf and the baby lay on it contentedly. It was a particularly happy morning, with no hint of trouble to come, but back in the house for lunch a storm suddenly burst. There was no obvious cause – a chance remark was enough, a fly, a mote, a nothing, but the peace of the day was shattered. My father shouted, the baby cried, my mother also cried, and my sister, snatching up the roaring child, assumed the role of a persecuted victim. 'I won't bear it any longer, you're hateful, I shall go home now at once. You can't stop me.' Of course she did not go and my mother eventually restored the calm, but it was an uneasy calm. My sister did not love or even like my father, though he loved her. She was his Dorothy, his gift from God (he chose all our names because of their meaning – Victorians were great on the language of names, the language of flowers, etc), and it was his sacred business to see that she jolly well was a gift from God, however badly she behaved to him.

It was my father's tragedy that, although so generous and affectionate, he was never able to achieve a satisfactory relationship with any of his children. Fortunately this was not to be the case with his grandchildren, who were all very fond of him and enjoyed his company. Perhaps this was because he mellowed with age, but I think it was more that he did not feel so responsible for them. He did, of course, care greatly about their spiritual welfare, but his concern was accepted by them and even indulged up to a point. True, one of them remarked once: 'I do wish Grandpa wouldn't talk to me about God while we are playing croquet, it puts me off my game.' But he never seemed to exasperate or oppress them in the same way as he had their parents.

Although I feared and hated the rows that blew up when my sister was at home, I was not above acrimonious argument with my father, which used to distress my mother. I could never keep my mouth shut as my brother had learned to do. Not every dispute, however, ended uncomfortably. I remember one on 'make-up'. My father had a deep distrust of the theatre and all things pertaining to it, including paint and powder, which he connected with an artificial and probably immoral world. I, of course, hotly defended make-up, though I had never yet dared to buy or use any. 'I think you will find,' said my father pontifically, 'that all good and virtuous girls . . .'. He paused to give his words a final authority, and I chipped in quickly, 'Powder their noses only,' and, unexpectedly, he laughed and changed the subject.

On the whole we got on together fairly well during this period. I was happy in my dreams of the future and he, always interested in history, liked to discuss it with me. We came together also in our joint efforts at land-work. As the war continued, the farmers became short of labour and there were not enough men on our farm to bring in the harvest. There were no combine harvesters then, and all the sheaves had to be stooked up by hand to dry. My father and I volunteered to help and between us tackled the large field behind the house. Eight sheaves went to the stook, six propped atainst each other in a row and one at each end. It was hard but satisfying work.

When we had finished this field we took on another near the sea and for our midday break climbed down the cliff by the rope ladder to a deserted shore and had a marvellously refreshing bathe before we ate our sandwiches. Close by there were the remains of a large coaster sunk by a German torpedo and, cast up by its side, a German submarine holed by a British destroyer. Both together were now equally given over to the waves and the crowds of brilliantly gleaming seagulls that hovered and cried ceaselessly about them.

After the corn had all been carried, the fields were golden with stubble and carpeted with flowers – my father's favourite poppies, and speedwell, flax, eyebright, milkwort, scarlet pimpernel, cornflowers, toadflax, and a host of others, while towards the sea were whole royal stretches of bugloss. Before these had all faded away ploughing began. There was a pair of horses at work in the fields that my father and I had helped to clear, but not far away, because horses too were in short supply, there was a team of oxen. Now, at the beginning of autumn, the sunsets were magnificent. I do not remember more glorious sunsets anywhere. By this time I had managed to dissociate these from the terror of the Last Judgement and was able to enjoy their copper and golden and turquoise and emerald splendour to the full. In a world which contained such skies, anything was possible.

The war, that had seemed an enduring part of life, looked as though at last it was drawing to its close (though still Wilfred Owen and many another had to die). Perhaps we would have peace before this Christmas and meanwhile, all before me, there was Oxford.

CHAPTER SEVEN

1918–1919
Oxford. First year up.

First of all I had to find my room. I was disappointed that it was in Old Hall, the white brick Victorian villa where LMH had begun forty years previously, but later I came to think this a privilege. There was no denying, however, that the room was unattractive, looking north on to the road and with a huge, hideous fireplace of brown and yellow tiles. Because of this, it was known as the Station Waiting Room – in those days stations had fireplaces like that. It contained a bed, a capacious oak wardrobe and chest of drawers, a writing table, two upright chairs and a washstand behind a green canvas screen. The washstand was furnished with a flowered China basin, jug, and chamber pot. Beside the fireplace hung three small oak shields engraved with the names of the former occupants. I gazed at these with awe and curiosity, noting with gratification that there was space on the third for my own name.

I unpacked, and hung over the solid marble mantelpiece my print of Rembrandt's *Knight in Armour* which I had chosen as a present from my father, and arranged my few books on the very big bookshelves that took up nearly all one wall. There were only Bryce and Voltaire's *Life of Charles XI of Sweden* (translated) in an Everyman edition, Erasmus's letters (a proscribed text), a Latin dictionary. A A Milne's *Once a Week*, Rupert Brook, and the *Oxford Book of English Verse*, which had been a parting gift from my housemistress at school. I hadn't particularly cared for her, but I owe her gratitude for this.

These volumes only took up half of one forlorn shelf, and

somehow managed to emphasize the bare look of the room. But I did not mind – it was the first room of my own, independent of my family, the first quite private room at the door of which people knocked before they came in. Precious privacy, how different from school where one had the worst of both worlds and was lonely in a crowd. Here I could be blessedly alone, but was never lonely for from the first there were plenty of knocks on my door.

There were twenty-five students in my year at LMH which was the largest year yet. I had come up with three others from my school (all to read History), which was a record. We went together that first day to pay our cheques to the Principal – £36 board and tuition for the term. She shook hands with us and gave us a brief welcome. She was Henrietta Jex Blake whose younger sister was Mistress of Girton and whose father had been Headmaster of Rugby. 'My father had us all taught Latin *and* Greek from the age of six.' Notwithstanding this, however, her interests were not academic, but musical. She played the violin well and there is a lovely portrait of her clasping her fiddle and looking happy. She was a stately woman and rather beautiful, and she dressed extremely well. But she was very shy and her shyness took the unfortunate form of a crisp curtness of manner which put off many people. It was difficult to maintain a conversation with her.

She gave uncomfortable duty tea parties at which one tried desperately to talk: 'I hope it won't be wet for Saturday's Garden Party, or worse still, neither one thing nor the other.' Principal: 'It must be either wet or fine'. End of conversation! Principal: 'And what have you been reading for amusement in the vacation?'

Me: 'Well, I've read Henry James's *Portrait of a Lady* which I liked very much.' Principal: 'Oh, you must be very young still.' End of conversation, and I still can't think what she meant by that. I think she was lonely as well as shy and not very happy in her position, but she held it valiantly through the war years, working hard and carrying out the duties of a secretary as well as a Principal and sacrificing much for the interests of the Hall.

It can't have been easy for Miss Jex Blake to follow Miss Wordsworth, the first Principal, who was in many ways an outstanding personality. It was she who had chosen the name – Lady Margaret, after the mother of Henry VII – and her reason for doing so was characteristically concisely and wittily expressed. 'She was a gentlewoman, a scholar, a saint, and after having been three times married she took a vow of celibacy. What more could have been expected of any woman?'

Miss Wordsworth was a great-niece of the poet, which in itself fascinated me, and I am glad I have a vivid memory of going to her house in Rawlinson Road for a Browning reading. We did not read much, for almost at once we came across a reference to a jerboa, and immediately the table became littered with natural history books, encyclopaedias, and maps, and we went away knowing more about the habitats of jerboas than of Browning. She was in her eighties and wore a cap (as all elderly ladies did then), but her face was alive with interest and intelligence. In my day her influence was still strong. It showed itself in the informal, friendly relationship between the dons and ourselves and a general sense of belonging to an extended family. Our number was small enough for us all to know each other.

A factor that strengthened the continuity with the past was that the Vice-Principal, Miss Lodge, had been one of Miss Wordsworth's early students and she was a dominant personality, not aggressively so, but through sheer benevolence and vitality. She was tall and spare, with a strong hawklike face, and she possessed boundless energy. It was said of her that one never knew whether she was having her night or her morning bath, she kept such late hours and got up so early. She was, I think, lucid and conscientious, rather than an inspiring tutor, but everyone liked her.

Every alternate Thursday evenings she kept open house in her room in Old Hall – one could come and go as one liked and the room was mostly full. At the end of term the whole Hall could and did crowd in and sit on the floor and sing and play games. It was she who really determined the tone of the place and this, as far as I could judge when I was up, was warmer, more friendly, and less critical than Somerville for instance. Less intellectual too, perhaps, and certainly less free-thinking.

LMH was founded as a Church of England college with a strongly religious bias. There was no bar operating against nonconformists, however, and my father was definitely in favour of a college with a chapel at which daily attendance was required, rather than one which was said to have agnostic, if not actually atheistic, tendencies. In my day the tradition of Christian Anglicanism was still a strong, cohesive element at the Hall, but I did not find this oppressive. Morning Chapel was taken for granted, in fact we kept our terms by signing our attendance, and evening worship was encouraged but voluntary.

One night, as the bell was sounding, I was making for the library when I met the Principal emerging from her room just opposite to officiate at the service. 'You are going the wrong way, I think,' she observed crisply. I agreed, but having an urgent essay to finish, I went on unabashed. But I would have missed having a chapel; even having it there to evade was a reassurance.

How lucky I was to have come up just at that particular meeting point of past and future in the history of the Hall and of women's education. The flavour of the first exciting beginning was still lingering on, some of the famous pioneers themselves – Miss Wordsworth, Mrs Johnson, Mrs Toynbee – still appeared on festive occasions like revered tribal deities, and at the end of my second year their fondest hopes were realized in the dawning of a new era when Oxford granted full university status to women. I could not have chosen a more interesting period.

But the start was inauspicious and sad. My year had not had time even to get to know each other's names before the vicious 1918 flu epidemic struck us. Nobody at first realized how deadly this was, but within a week almost all the students and most of the dons had succumbed.

I had had just one coaching while life was yet normal. My tutor for European history was Evelyn Jamison who, like Miss Lodge, was an old student of the Hall. It was said of her that she had been viva'd for over an hour in her Finals just for the pleasure it gave the examiners to hear her talk. I think it may also have been for the pleasure of looking at her, for she was very handsome. When I knew her she was arresting, with one white lock of hair among the dark brown, swept back in a wave from her forehead. I was paired off for her tutorials with the History scholar of our year, Joan Luard, whom I had known fairly well at school and whom I greatly liked and admired. She was clever, humble, humorous, and brave. Together, during our first week, we crossed the lawns to our tutor's room one afternoon, full of mutual trepidation and excitement. I was to remember that coaching all my life for it was the only one I was to have with Joan.

Two days later I had my first tutorial in English History with Miss Lodge, which did not last long. 'You've got it,' she exclaimed suddenly and, darting across the room, thrust a thermometer into my mouth. True enough, my temperature was up and I was packed off at once to my 'station waiting room' and bed. I think every single student in Old Hall was smitten, but luckily our two resident dons – Miss Lodge and her great friend, Miss Spens, the English don, escaped and between them they nursed us all. There was no treatment but bed and aspirin and I did not see a doctor – they were reserved for the serious cases, of which there were many. I remember thinking that probably nothing like this had been experienced in Oxford since the Plague of 1665 – the bells were continually tolling.

Our floor was looked after by Miss Spens (Spenny), who was probably the least practical of all the dons, but she was very conscientious and kind. She was small and frail, with great expressive grey eyes and wispy fair hair. She wandered in and out of my room like a gentle ghost, bringing me hot milk and more aspirin, and she beamed approval when I asked for my *Oxford Book of English Verse.*

I had been ill for a little while when a knock came at my door and, much to my surprise, the Principal appeared. She came in silently and sat down. Then she said: 'I am afraid I have some very bad news for you.' It could only have been a moment or two before she spoke again, but it was long enough for me to think in terror of my mother, my brother, and my baby niece. But it was Joan. Hating to give in, and ignorant of the fatal tendency of this flu to develop into pneumonia, she had held out against it too long and was already very ill when she finally collapsed and was taken to the little Hospice off Norham Road where there were slightly better facilities for nursing than at the Hall. But she had died three days later.

The poor Principal must have been harassed and miserable. She, too, was nursing students for all she was worth, and was, I believe, very efficient at it, but she was not much good at condolence and I was glad when she left me alone. I felt very shaken and sad, especially for Joan's devoted sister and mother, both of whom I knew. Her father had been killed in the war. Her sister wrote, 'Don't mind so much. Joan is with my father now and must be so happy.' But she had been very happy here, in the garden that day on our way to her coaching with me, and life would be the poorer without her.

As soon as we were well enough we were all sent off in pairs to neighbouring villages to convalesce. I went to Boars Hill to the one hotel in the quietly remote woods. It was small and friendly and the food was good, at least it seemed so to me, for my standards after four years of war were not high. I gained strength quickly and went for walks, proud and entranced by the distant views of Oxford across the fields. After a week I was well enough to go back. It was midday on November 11th, though I did not know how significant this date was, for I had no newspaper (and of course no radio!). But the taxi that had been ordered to take me to the Hall had to slow up outside Christ Church because of the crowds in the street, all shouting and waving. My driver turned round grinning at me. 'The

war's over,' he said. Some of the people climbed onto the roof
as we proceeded slowly up Cornmarket and into the Broad.
There we shed them. That night the Roman heads round the
Sheldonian were painted scarlet. They remained pink for quite
a long while.

Arriving at the Hall eventually, I found that a party for our
Fresher year was being organized to celebrate the armistice
and to exchange our names at last. This was a gathering at the
Oak Tearooms opposite Trinity and next door to the house
where Yeats was living. A tea-party in a mock Tudor tea room
– how tame and dull that sounds, but it was a splendid party
– so full of hope. Hope indeed was in the air all about us.
Oxford was emerging from the desert of war. The
rehabilitation of colleges and the Examination Schools, which
had been taken over for hospitals, had begun. (LMH had
escaped this fate and had only had to dig up its tennis courts to
plant potatoes.) University life had been maintained during the
war years almost entirely by the women students but now,
though demobilization was slow, everywhere began to bur-
geon with undergraduates again. In January 1919 I wrote
home triumphantly 'Balliol is quite full this term and Oriel has
80 freshers.'

These formed two distinct groups – the war veterans and the
school leavers. To a lesser degree this division was also
noticeable in the women's colleges. Deeper than the obvious
differences of age, there was a contrast of mood and maturity.
Actually, I do not recollect being much conscious of this at the
time, certainly not in my own immediate circle but, on reading
Vera Britten's *Testament of Youth*, I realize now how wide was
the gap. The predominant atmosphere that I remember was
that of release, confidence, and idealism. Many of us really
believed that the war had been a war to end wars, we really
believed that now the country would get down to providing
homes for heroes, that a fresh spirit of justice and equality was
abroad, and we really believed that the newly-formed League
of Nations would ensure peace.

Bliss was it in that day to be alive,
And to be young was very heaven.

Wordsworth wrote this at the dawn of the French Revolution and round the corner was the Reign of Terror and the Napoleonic Wars. Round our corner was the dole queue, the general strike, and Hitler.

War conditions, of course, did not vanish with the signing of the Armistice. Food was still in short and dull supply, and if you were late for a meal you were apt to find nothing left. What was available lacked variety. The Principal was heard to remark once, 'I shall never be able to encounter a haricot bean again for the rest of my life without a shudder.'

It was also cold that winter. There was nothing but open fires to heat our rooms, and we were allowed only one small bucket of coal every other day. We accepted this state of things as inevitable, sharing our fires, working in each other's rooms, and supplementing our meals whenever we could afford it at the Oak Tearooms, the Cadena, or the School of Cookery in the Broad.

My first term was already half over before I got down to my work properly and I found it taxing. I enjoyed some of the lectures, especially those of rubicund, burly Prof Marriot, who started declaiming before he got into the lecture room, but Constitutional History, which chiefly consisted of ploughing through old 'Stubbs', I found daunting and dull, and the amount of Latin required for the Previous was alarming. However life in general was unbelievably entertaining. To be free of compulsory games and, instead, to explore the countryside on legs or bicycles and the river in boats was pure joy. One had to be coached for the river, though, as quite difficult tests had to be passed in sculling, punting, and canoeing before being allowed to take a boat out. This was a challenge I set myself at once, for had not my brother captained his college boat at Cambridge.

One day I was on my way to the boat house when, on the river path, I met the fresher who had taken Joan's place after the flu epidemic. I had not come across her before. She told me afterwards that she had taken an immediate dislike to me. 'Always a good sign,' she added, 'for I nearly always find later that I was wrong.' There was perhaps some justification this time, because I was feeling sad about Joan and may have regarded her coldly. It was nonetheless an epoch in both our lives, for she was to become dearer to me than either of my sisters and our close friendship ended only with her death nearly sixty-five years later.

Evelyn was reading English and I soon found other kindred spirits among the English students. I envied them their poets and Stubbs became less and less attractive.

At the beginning of my second term I wrote home as follows:

'I have done a rather tremendous thing – it had to be done quickly or I should probably have told you first. I have changed from the History to the English school. My heart was really with English all the time. Well, on Friday I heard that it was just possible to change and I have thought and thought about it, all for and against. What really decided me was what suddenly seemed to come home to me. When I've got my degree, what am I to do with it? Am I all my life to work at something which I only like second best? Horrible! What is the use of wasting such a splendid opportunity which you are giving to me. And is it better to get a third class in history or do pretty well in English? My lack of Latin and French (for I am not good at either) means that I have to work hard at them to the detriment of my actual history. Well, I went to 'Slodge' for my coaching after all this thought, and she seemed so pleased with my last essay that I simply couldn't broach the subject for I thought she might be annoyed; meanwhile I had been told by a third year that if one tried to change schools it was most unpopular, and on Saturday I was in despair. All history seemed flat, stale, and unprofitable but that evening Miss Spens, the

English don, asked me if I could find time to go to a
Browning reading once a week. This seemed to me a
direct opportunity (especially as I had been praying for
one), and so I poured out everything to her. She was
extremely nice and thought it might be managed, and she
would talk to Miss Lodge that night. I begged her not to
let Miss Lodge think for a moment that she had made
history dull for me (nor had she, but I hadn't realized
fully before that political science and constitutional
history are just drudgery for me). Miss L. saw me this
morning and was thoroughly kind and sound as is her
nature. She said she would be sorry to lose me but I was
right to follow my real bent *if* I was quite sure. The
Principal will be furious – she hates people to change and
she doesn't like the English school, but I don't mind her
in the very least and if Miss Lodge says I may change she
can't say 'no'. Do write soon and tell me if you think I've
done right.'

Actually it was easier in one way to change schools then, as
degrees were not yet granted to women, and so it did not really
make much difference if one skipped an intermediate exam
and read only for finals. This I determined to do to make up
for my lost term. All the same I had quite a struggle. My
parents were a bit dubious, friends disapproved, and the
Principal was peevish. 'You would do far better to remain in
the History School.' English was looked upon then as a poor
relation. It had no 'Previous' of its own, for instance, and was
a comparatively new subject at Oxford. We had a song we used
to sing about it, adapted from the Mikado:

> An English student I, a thing of little moment.
> My syllabus is long, continually changing
> Through every period ranging,
> And so we rub along, and so we rub along.

I never regretted the change and in a later letter wrote, 'I know

I did right. I am blissfully happy altogether now. My coachings, however, are far more of an intellectual strain than my history coaching was. I have horrible questions fired at me, such as 'What is your theory of love?' 'What do you mean by beauty?' etc.'

What I should have liked best would have been a combination of literature and social history instead of the prescribed Anglo-Saxon, but one can't have everything.

My first essay for Miss Spens was on Wordsworth. 'Any special aspect?' I enquired tentatively. 'No dear – just Wordsworth', and 'just Wordsworth' it was for one week, but it could as easily have been for the whole term. No-one could have called my tutor practical. A classic remark of hers immediately before my finals was a casual: 'You know your Homer, of course?' 'Not really,' I confessed. 'Well then, I do think it would be just worth your while to run through him, preferably in the original, before your schools.'

Her lectures were apt to be rambling and discursive and she was not a popular lecturer. 'It is a rather horrible experience, dearie,' she would say sadly, 'to see one's audience melt away as term progresses until there are only two or three poor souls left.' Then she would give one of her unexpected guffaws which seemed to shake her whole small, frail body. But her coachings were never in the least dull, always stimulating and attentive to one's particular needs. She cared about her pupils as individuals and, when I came to teach, I drew constantly on her inspiration and example. She taught me, if not to be a scholar, at least what scholarship meant. She had her prejudices of course. 'I do not think we will trouble ourselves about Restoration Drama dearie, a rather nasty period.' She was at her best on the Romantics and Elizabethans, and had published a very good book on Spenser.

I began to enjoy my work greatly. Exams were far off now and, for the first time for years, pressure was lifted from me. One evening I sat late in the Library finishing an essay on 'just' Keats, the room empty and dusk falling. My reading lamp sent a glow upon the picture hanging above the fireplace. It was an old oil painting of cattle and dark, brooding trees. From the window I could see out across the silent meadows to the willows and the still faintly luminous river. The immemorial trees and cattle in the picture, the landscape outside, Keats, and myself were all fused together for one eternal marvellous moment. I wrote my final sentence and was pleased with it. Over in Old Hall firelight and friendship were waiting for me. I packed up my books, awed by an immense joy.

In the Easter vac I went to stay with Evelyn at her home near Abingdon. This house and its household became better known to me over the years than any other except my own, and it was even more redolent of a lost world. Northcourt House was a large, gracious, red-brick Georgian building, very solid look-ing and comfortable, surrounded by lawns separated from farm land by a 'ha ha'. It was a rather grander house than any that I had stayed in before and I was impressed to find my bag all unpacked for me and my evening dress laid out on my bed. The maid had also brought me a ewer of hot water, and folded a towel over it. She did this four times a day, for though the house could sleep ten or more there was only one bathroom, though that contained the biggest bath I have ever known. The polished brass ewers stood like a battalion, row upon row on the top of a landing cupboard.

Everyone assembled before dinner in the drawing room, which had a blue Morris wallpaper and many pictures – several by Evelyn's sister Agnes, who exhibited yearly at the Royal Academy. These were portraits of the family or subject painting in the pre-Raphaelite style, and I admired them greatly. They were indeed good of their kind and are now sought after. The curtains at the big windows were also William Morris and two hung over a door into a conservatory full of ferns and geraniums.

We filed into the dining room in state. This had more of Agnes's pictures but was dominated by a splendid and very good reproduction of Raphael's *Madonna with the Goldfinch*. I sat next to Evelyn's father. He had a walrus moustache, like my own father, and very bushy eyebrows which he had occasionally to brush out of his eyes. He was a sensitive, gentle, and most courteous man, a classical scholar with an impish, delightful turn of humour, though given at times to melancholy and anxiety from which he was rescued by his cheerful, wise wife.

Mr Tatham had private pupils, amongst whom were at one time Maurice Baring (the novelist) and Ivor Brown (the Shakespearean critic). All his pupils remembered him with gratitude. When I first knew him he had almost given up teaching, though he was still an active JP and church warden. I was more at ease with him at first than with Mrs Tatham, who, though always kind to me was, I felt (probably mistakenly), inclined to criticize or rather to dismiss as irrelevant anyone outside her large family circle.

I found Northcourt House more ordered and conventional a house than my own, also more polite and reserved and therefore (to me at any rate) more restful and attractive, but it had enough in common to reassure me and to make me feel at home. Mr Tatham, like my father, was a Gladstonian Liberal and, like him also, was public-spirited and sincerely religious though without his uncomfortable fervour. Both Mr Tatham and the eldest daughter, Silvia, spent time and energy on 'good works', as did my mother and aunt. They too took Bible classes and ran girl's clubs, and Mrs Tatham regularly visited the grim-looking Abingdon Workhouse and gave Workhouse parties. There was the same importance attached to the arts by both families, though the Tathams had a longer tradition behind them. It was a Tatham who was a friend of Samuel Palmer and John Linnell. I learnt now much more about painting and pictures than I had known before.

There were probably not more books about the house than at home, but there were certainly far more in beautiful bindings and beautiful bookcases. As for music, Mrs Tatham and Agnes sometimes played piano duets in the evening, though Evelyn and her father were even less musical than my mother. He could not recognize the National Anthem unless people stood up for it. It is perhaps typical that there was no gramophone.

The day began, as at home, with Family Prayers, shorter and more formal than my father's. Then, directly after our very substantial breakfast, we rushed upstairs, a beautiful stairway curling round a tall oval window and flanked by walls thickly crowded with photographs in oak frames. We were making for the old schoolroom at the top of the house. Here the life of the three sisters was carried on when they were at home. Silvia, the eldest, did not seem to me to belong to the younger generation at all, and she had her own sitting-room below.

I loved the schoolroom. It was large and light with two huge windows and white shelves full of bound copies of Punch, and the gold and scarlet works of E Nesbit, and the blue novels of Charlotte Yonge, and dark red sets of Scott and Dickens, and big volumes of reproductions of Italian Renaissance paintings. There was a red and blue Turkey carpet, and a square table replete with an inkstand and an overflowing pen and pencil tray. There were two armchairs (one upholstered in worn red velvet) drawn up before the fireplace in which there was already a cheerfully-blazing fire (the coal shortage seems to have been over by now, at any rate at Northcourt House). In front of the fire was a high brass-rimmed nursery fireguard on which one could comfortably cock up one's legs when lounging in the chairs. Along the whole mantlepiece was a row of miniature china houses, the walls were hung with more of Agnes's pictures, and there was a corner cupboard housing a fine collection of china cats.

In this room we spent all the time we were not out bicycling or on the river. It was a lovely March that year. One day we took a picnic into Bagley Woods, and there among the primroses we confessed our love for one another. This does not mean what everybody today would think. We had never heard of lesbianism and I did not then, nor indeed ever, feel any sort of physical attraction to Evelyn, and though later I was conscious that something was lacking in our relationship, I did not know what it was that I had needed until I fell in love with my husband. What happened on this particular spring day, however, was unforgettable and as near a declaration of first love as makes no matter. It was a true exchange of trust, a mutual give and take of mind and heart, and for the time being it was completely satisfying.

From Abingdon I went to join my parents who were having a short holiday in Bath. In spite of the charm of the place and of Jane Austen's *Persuasion* with which my father presented me on arrival and which I read in those most appropriate surroundings for the first time, I missed my friends badly, wrote long letters to Evelyn, and argued and laid down the law to both my poor parents until even my mother's patience was exhausted.

'You're unbearable!' she exclaimed. '*Me*, unbearable!? Surely not!' This brought me up short.

I was glad when we went home to Hodcombe and began to count the time till I was due back at LMH for the Summer term. But when the day came (it happened to be April 25th, the auspicious date of my birth) I woke to find the Downs all covered with snow and the roads impassable (I remember only two other birthdays in snow). There was nothing for it but to wait for it to melt, which it did in time for me to travel safely to Oxford the next day. At the station I was lucky and secured the one hansom cab, always much sought after, and I swung up St Giles and along to Norman Gardens in fine style. All my friends seemed to be assembled in my room which they had filled with flowers to greet me. None but myself had been snowed up, but now the freak return of winter was quite over and I was wearing a new summer outfit, a blue and white frilled, spotted dress and a little round straw hat with a navy ribbon (the nearest I ever got to my childhood's dream of a sailor suit). The sun was shining and it seems now to have shone all that term, for the two months that followed were a lyrical period like no other in my life. I do not mean that it was the time of my deepest joy, but it was certainly the most unallayed and carefree, unshadowed by any sort of strain or responsibility. Sometimes at night in bed, I used to hug myself for happiness.

I had discovered that the best gift that Oxford had to offer was the opportunity to make rich, splendid friendships. This was, I think, something that was not yet just taken for granted by women: our mothers had not enjoyed it. Their friendships for the most part had been limited to the family and to those chosen for them by their parents. For myself, I realized that hitherto I had often been lonely, though it was only the wealth of congenial companionship now at hand that made this clear to me. My friends were many and varied, a fact that was commented on by my tutor, and they did not always mix together quite comfortably. But that only added a spice to life. I think no-one ever could have had better friends. The bonds forged between us during those short years lasted a lifetime. It is not that other later friendships have been less dear, but the ties of these earlier ones have been almost like blood ties. Nothing that one could do or say, nothing that might happen, could alter them. Founded on a shared morning, they have withstood the busy day and the marauding night.

But my business now is with the morning:

"How light we were, how right we were
How fair faith shone."

Everything was starting up again. That summer was the occasion of the first 'Eights' week since the War, with splendid teas on the college barges, strawberries and cream and ices, not seen for ages past. Tennis Mondays at LMH were also reinstituted that term, when undergraduates were allowed to play with us, though there had to be a chaperone on duty. This, indeed, was the last year of the chaperone but the rules, though tottering, were still observed. If you were invited out to one of the men's colleges a chaperone had to accompany you; if you entertained an undergraduate it must not be in your room but in one of the Common rooms with a don as a fellow guest. It was both tiresome and embarrassing to have to book a poor, unwilling don for these occasions. This term though there was one concession. If you made up your party to more than two, you were allowed to entertain in the garden unattended.

None of these rules bothered me. I knew only three undergraduates, and of these found only one interesting. He was Jack Collis, one of three brothers, each of whom made a name for themselves.* Jack invited me for a river picnic to which I took as chaperone poor Miss McCutcheon, the classics don, who, for some reason I have forgotten, was an easy prey. The friendship with Jack, however, did not prosper until much later. I was shy of him, and at the moment I did not feel the need for any male companionship. I was more than satisfied with my women friends, and I had my brother.

He came up for a glorious weekend. At last his demobilization had come through and he was on the look-out for a wife and a job. Not long after this he confided to me that he had fallen in love with a medical student, 'Just what I had vowed to myself I would never do!' When I met her I did not wonder at him, for she was a beautiful, Irish girl with blue eyes and dark hair and a Leonardo-shaped face, and was sensitive and clever besides, but alas, with very poor health. They were married the following year. That weekend I felt very close to him. He had become a great reader during the war and was interested in my work. I did not possess a Shakespeare of my own and he gave me one – a three volume edition printed on Indian paper and specially bound for me. We chose the binding together, half calf with green leather labels. The big shelves in my room were by now decently filled and I added the Shakespeare with love and pride.

This term I was no longer coaching by myself, but had been paired off with another student. At first I was annoyed by this, but I soon changed my mind. Ethel (who became another close lifelong friend) had a fine critical intelligence. She went deeper

* Jack and Maurice as writers, Robert Collis as a doctor involved in rescue work for children in German concentration camps after the Second World War.

into a subject and set a higher standard than my own more superficial approach. She met life with intensity tempered by humour. You couldn't be dull with her, and my tutorials became twice as lively. Also we now only had to produce, alternately, one essay per week. This meant that every other week I could spend peacefully browsing among my books at my own pace. Exams were so far off as to be practically non-existent, and Anglo-Saxon was, I am ashamed to say, as yet nothing but a joke. So work was pure enjoyment and, to crown all, we were 'doing' the Elizabethans. Sidney's *Arcadia* and Spenser's *Faery Queen* were forever identified for me with the water meadows of the Cherwell, as I lay among the buttercups and the flowering may, or under an old apple tree by the river path, while all the birds sang.

I did not bother much with lectures, but there were certain ones I never missed. The life and soul of the English School then was Walter Raleigh. He was in fact the first to be appointed Professor of the Oxford School of Literature and he gave it shape and structure. He was adored by his students, and every week he filled the large, tiered lecture room of the University Museum to overflowing. His warmth, enthusiasm, and wide interests appealed to us strongly, as also did his engaging informality. He had an arresting appearance. Abnormally tall and thin with a long, bony face and high forehead, he looked like some Gothic stone figure stepped down from a Cathedral niche, but no-one could have been less pontifical or even 'donnish'. He possessed a superb voice, mellow and flexible, which he used to great advantage when sharing with us his favourite passages. I recall especially passages from A E Houseman, Meredith's *Love in a Valley*, and the Lyke Wake Dirge.

He laced his often profound and creative criticism with casual asides – the sort of comments we loved. I have some of them in old lecture notes still, copiously illustrated with sketches of undergraduates in the margin.

'The one poem in Shelley's family before his own was written by his grandmother:

It was not my wish to call him Bysshe
It was only the whim of his Uncle Tim.'

'A public lecture on Charles Lamb! He would not have approved and nor do I.'

'The final honours school and the Day of Judgment are two events not one.'

'Remember to read always for *fun*.'

He did not really approve of examinations, especially for women. In fact, though he was always particularly nice to them, I doubt if he much approved of women at the University at all. He had an all-embracing zest for life which makes it particularly ironic that his best-known rhyme is the misanthropic 'I wish I loved the human race', which was probably written after a particularly dull don's tea party. He had something of the adventurous spirit of his famous Elizabethan namesake, and it was this and the fact that he had had three sons serving in the forces that led to him accepting with great pleasure the commission to write the history of Britain's airforce during the 1914–18 war. It was during the visit to Baghdad while at work on this that he caught typhoid and died in 1922.

Literature for him was part of the adventure of living. I suppose his books on Shakespeare and Milton were the most popular. He disliked Milton's puritanism and liked to quote Houseman's: 'Malt does more than Milton can, to justify God's ways to man.' But no-one has praised Milton better. My favourites among his writings, however, are his six essays on Johnson, for they gave me Johnson as a friend for life.

During this Elysian term, our weekly language sessions with dear, gentle Mrs Wright put no sort of pressure on me to take Anglo-Saxon seriously. Her husband, Joseph Wright, was another notable Oxford character. The son of a ne'er do-well Yorkshire miner, he had, by his own efforts, become Professor of Philology, and had called into being and edited *The English Dialect Dictionary*. He had also produced an Anglo-Saxon grammar which I found baffling in the extreme. He was a big, genial man, and I remember him enquiring people's names and then booming out the part of the country they came from. He himself was proud of being a Yorkshire man, their house in the Banbury Road was called 'Thackley' after the Yorkshire village in which he was born. Mrs Wright, an early LMH student, had been one of his pupils and they entertained at 'Thackley' on Sunday afternoons. But all his geniality and her sweetness could not dispel the sadness that haunted their home, for they had lost both the little son and daughter whose enlarged, heavily-framed photographs dominated every room. I could not *then* appreciate the full depth of this tragedy, not the courage with which they faced it, but I felt it as a background to our classes and teas at 'Thackley'.

I began my first long vac with a series of visits. Of my close Oxford friends, three had lost fathers, four had happy family backgrounds, and three others had parents who taught me to value my own more highly by contrast. At Ethel's home, I felt unhappy for her, though admiring her all the more for being what she was. Her father bullied her timid, pretty, dim mother unmercifully, and tyrannized his five children, not for the good of their souls like my own father, but to feed his own ego. He was a successful businessman who had had a hard and poverty-haunted childhood. Everything in their big Edwardian house at Kenilworth was expensive, ordinary, and dangerous, for to damage any object even slightly was treated as a crime. I thought that Ethel was joking when she wrung her hands over a tiny mark on a polished table, but it was no joke, as I discovered to my amazement. Ethel got her brains from her father, but where her fierce love of truth and beauty came from, I don't know. She had achieved Oxford through the influence of a kind and intelligent teacher and it had been a rescue operation.

After this visit came the conference of the Student Christian Movement at Swanwick. The SCM had an active following at LMH then, and Evelyn and I were both on the Committee. I had found that my parents' influence was active when I was away from them, and it had seemed only natural to join the

movement, just as it did to attend the Presbyterian Church or
Mansfield Chapel* every Sunday. Religion which, when I was
emerging from childhood, had first troubled and then comforted me, became at this period an intellectual rather than an
emotional concern. Like almost everything else, it interested
me enormously.

The SCM was engaged in changing its aim and basis and
moving towards a more liberal attitude. Evelyn and I found
the Swanwick conference rather too hearty for our liking, but
we were impressed by large, genial Neville Talbot and Canon
Barnes of the Temple who later became the liberal-minded
Bishop of Birmingham. We thought it our duty to support the
new approach, and next term started a group to study the ideas
that had been put forward at the conference. We certainly took
ourselves seriously, if no-one else did.

I described my efforts to my parents in a moving passage:

> Our study group was quite helpful I think, though it is very
> difficult to lead – to draw out, connect and sympathize with
> other people's ideas, to keep one's own clear, to stop people
> from getting off the point and yet to encourage them to
> discuss. The worst difficulty is the varying intellects we seem
> to have collected in the group.

But obviously I enjoyed it all, as I had enjoyed the experience
of Swanwick, with no more qualms and questionings than
served to enliven life.

When I rejoined my parents after the conference, it was not
at Hodcombe, which was being enlarged and provided with a
bathroom and indoor sanitation, but at the nearby Manor
Farm where we were lodging until the improvements were
finished. There had been a homestead here from Saxon times
and the present house dated from the 16th century. It was a
lovely, mellow building lying in a fold of the Downs with a
golden lichen-covered roof and a big walled garden. But when

* The nonconformist theological college

we were staying there it was all rather shabby and neglected. It had obviously seen better days and was, I am glad to say, to see them again.

The tenant farmer and his two spinster sisters appeared slightly sinister to me; the women hardly ever spoke, but flitted about the place disapproving of us and of their brother. He was still courting Elsie, the village shopkeeper's daughter, and was still not allowed to bring her into the house. Altogether there was 'a cold comfort farmish' sort of atmosphere around. I shut myself up in my small, stuffy bedroom and tried to work. But I was suffering from a worse reaction even than during the previous vac. I could not sleep and felt frightened of some unknown menace and wrote long letters to my brother and to all my friends. With my propensity for reading the wrong book for the mood and the time, I was now deep in *Wuthering Heights*. I felt better when it was finished and we were back in our own house with Oxford drawing near once more.

CHAPTER EIGHT

1919–1921
Oxford continued

A different sort of happiness was waiting for me there – busier and wider in interests, if less lyrical. My second year saw a leap forward in the emancipation of women, with the fading away of chaperones to the glorious granting of full university status. There were small but significant signs among us, such as the bobbing of hair and greater freedom in our clothing. I was not yet one of those adventurous spirits who parted with their hairpins and coils, but I rejoiced in the quite new fashion of knitted jumpers or pullovers. For the first time since I wore elastic blouses I was relieved from the burden of keeping tidy around my waist. We all proudly sported these newfangled jumpers that winter, mostly knitted by our mothers, As far as I can remember, no-one had more than one and I could even now assign to each of my friends her particular colour and pattern. We never seemed to wear anything else, except in the evenings. Then I exchanged my grey and blue jumper for a dark red dress trimmed with grey squirrel fur, in which I fancied myself, and marched into Hall for our formal 'dinner', which, as I told my parents, 'had improved in quantity though not yet in quality.'

We lived very simply and never thought of doing otherwise. For instance, no-one dreamed of drinking anything but water at mealtimes, and cocoa brewed afterwards in our rooms. My personal expenses seem to have been covered by £10 a term. My father had started me off with a bank account, and I kept careful accounts, and I think my standards were about average. No-one of course owned a car, and bicycles were the cheap and universal form of transport. They were also fairly common property. Ethel seldom had her own.

We were still coaching together, but this autumn Janet Spens was having a term off and we were to have a man to coach us. This excited us at first. We hung out of my window to get a look at him when he called to see Spenny. 'He is quite young,' I wrote to my mother 'not more than 35 I should imagine. Think of *that* for an Oxford don!' But he was a great disappointment. 'He wears tan suede boots and strides up and down pouring forth his ideas, cribbed mostly from other people, on every subject under the sun. He never listens to our essays and we now write just for each other.' A later letter dismisses him summarily: 'No, I am afraid we are *not* prejudiced against Mr W, we try very hard about him, but he does not like us to have our own opinions. It's no use dwelling on him, I've only four more coachings and then no more Mr W next term, thank you!'

We were more indulgent to little, ancient Prof Craigie, to whom Spenny sent us for Icelandic literature, which was not part of our syllabus and in which neither of us, I am afraid, was at all interested. 'I do hope you won't mind,' Spenny said apologetically, 'but I *can't* disappoint Mr Craigie, he does *so* want to give these lectures, and I can't think of anyone to send him but you two.' So obediently off we rode on our bikes once a week, climbed a narrow stairway in a house next to Blackwells in the Broad (now swept away to provide further Bodleian Library space), and sat ourselves down, the only two occupants of a dark little room, where we waited until the gnome-like figure of Prof Craigie arrived and beamed at us across a sheaf of lecture notes. It was an innocent, if fruitless, hour for all three.

I was working harder this year and also taking more part in Hall and inter-collegiate societies. I joined the Liberal Club and the College Debating Society. 'Last week there was a debate on the Trial of the Kaiser. I spoke against it twice and I am glad to say that only seven people voted for the trial.' A great occasion was the first ever joint debate with one of the men's colleges – St Johns, I think it was. I was one of the four set speakers, and the subject was 'The future of Constantinople – should it continue under Turkish rule?' I certainly knew nothing to justify such an undertaking, but hastily looked up some facts and got through it somehow. I remember that I was very nervous, and that the Principal complimented me on not being nervous at all in a voice that implied that it would have been more becoming in me at least to have appeared so. I also joined the newly-formed League of Nations Union and wrote home enthusiastically of a meeting in the Town Hall. 'It was splendid, Lord Hugh Cecil spoke first and I liked what he said and how he said it. After him two Bishops and Dr Selbie of Mansfield and then Prof Gilbert Murray and all were good.'

I think this was my first encounter with Gilbert Murray (Regius Professor of Greek), who became another dominating influence. He was very friendly with Janet Spens, who had been a student of his at Glasgow, and because of this friendship and the fact that I became Secretary of the LMH branch of the LNU, I sometimes met him personally. But it was his reading of Greek and English poetry that enchanted me. I hastened to share my enthusiasm with my mother:

After I had finished my last letter to you I went to a most interesting meeting. It was a WEA* meeting at the Friends Meeting House where Prof Murray was lecturing on Shelley. Gilbert Murray quoting Shelley is the very essence of poetry and music combined. There followed a rather dreadful discussion in which people made fatuous remarks – one of them was a man who had interrupted the LNU meeting by shouting 'Anarchy for ever!' Then suddenly Mr Asquith rose up from a row just behind us and proposed a vote of thanks. I had not noticed him before. He looked very ill and tired, I thought, but it was a relief to listen to him and he gave a delightful short appreciation of Murray. The

---

* The recently formed Workers' Educational Association

Seconder though was pretty bad. He remarked that, though it was nice to have such great men among them as Prof Murray and Mr Asquith, they would be just as happy and interested, he was sure, at the next meeting when they would be on their own. Hardly the thing to say when seconding a vote of thanks.

Murray's sympathy with Shelley was deep, and sprang from a natural affinity with his platonic philosophy. Some people have the knack of appearing exactly the sort of person they are. No-one could have looked more like a romantic poet than Shelley, and Gilbert Murray's keen, aquiline features were reminiscent of a classical statue. Shelley, however, is reported as having an unattractive voice, whereas Murray's was a beautiful tenor. Spenny persuaded him to give a course of lectures on Greek Drama especially for the English School. There were a revelation to me. He would first read or recite the original Greek, and it was better even than hearing him quote Shelley. I thought of him as Hermes, the Messenger of the Gods, for hitherto I had known little or nothing of Greek literature. I wished I was reading classics. The idealism of Murray's political philosophy also appealed to me and I worked quite hard for the LNU.

My education continued to widen. Partly owing to the war, partly due to my Puritan background, I had been to few plays or concerts and so enjoyed any that I now experienced all the more intensely. Two OUDS performances were specially memorable. The production of Antony and Cleopatra was perhaps unique in that the undergraduate acting Antony had fallen deeply in love with his Cleopatra – young Cathleen Nesbitt (it was her first major Shakespearian part). She, too, was carried away, for he was very good-looking and spoke beautifully. They were afterwards married, so that what we were seeing was the real thing. Then there was Hardy's *Dynasts*, most appropriate to our post-war mood and with Hardy himself in the audience, frail and white-haired, responding from his box to our cheers with a bow and a wave of the hand, though refusing to make a speech.

In Gilbert and Sullivan week we did little work, queueing each afternoon for the gallery and then, immediately on coming out of the theatre, turning round and queueing again for the evening performance. Alas, I could have had much more music than came my way had I realized what opportunities were there for the asking. But my circle of friends were none of them musicians, and I was unaware till later of the musical centre at Gunfield, the home of the Deneke family, which was next door to Old Hall and frequented by Vaughan Williams amongst other great musical personalities. I had a try at the Bach choir which was performing his *Sea Symphony*, but fierce Sir Hugh Allen frightened me and I knew I wasn't really good enough. But I was carried away by the performance for which my kind tutor gave me a ticket. Altogether, life was very full and through all my work and all my leisure, friendship flowed like a bright stream.

By this time I had acquired a south-facing room overlooking Old Hall garden and the big trees bordering the university parks. It had a William Morris wallpaper of tiny grey leaves and red berries. I loved this room. Evelyn who, when she laughed (which she often did), screwed up her eyes until they disappeared and poured with tears, used to amuse herself by writing skits upon my habits and behaviour. The least libellous of these was about this room. It was called 'Space'.

She left me on the tennis court and I found her half an hour later in her room in a vague and happy dream. But I hadn't much thought to give to her, the room immediately claimed all my critical and wondering attention. There was an immediate impression of emptiness. Most of the furniture had disappeared and the usually crowded window sill was bare – the large table pushed into the far corner empty except for one row of books and a pen. In the centre of the room the small table stood as usual, holding only an immensely tall thin plant. I turned to see her still removing thing after thing and putting them behind her screen which was perilously elongated. She opened the windows wide and required me to join with her in her ecstasy upon space.

We stood and *felt* how glorious it was for some minutes, but there was more work to be done. She took me to look behind the screen, carrying with her the wastepaper basket and the coal scuttle. There I found much of the missing articles. She was obviously delighted at the difficulty there would be about dressing and getting to her chest of drawers. When we settled down to work in the empty part of the room which now consisted of all except the small triangle hidden by the screen, she, as usual, impressed me with her desire for silence and continuous concentration. After a short pause, the happy dream still on her face, she began:

'There's plenty of room, isn't there?'

Then minutes later I was woken from my preoccupation with Beowulf by a worried voice:

'I never knew my wardrobe took up so much space before.'

Innocently I suggested that she should keep it in my room or give it up altogether, and keep her clothes horizontally in layers under her bed. She thought this over for a few minutes and then discarded the suggestions. Later the dream voice again:

'Don't you *love* having it all *bare* round you?'

Then again, with happy pride,

'It *will* be rather difficult opening my chest of drawers.'

Later the voice became a little worried:

'Do you think *anyone* would exchange a smaller table for mine?'

I tried a little conversation on my own account but obviously tonight we might talk only of space.

Evelyn teased but she also cherished me far beyond my desserts. It is true that I have always loved space, but paradoxically I am also a hoarder. Out of an old notebook the other day fell a scribbled note apparently passed to me more than sixty years ago, during a lecture.

For my poor dear who has had two days of wearisome toothache, here is a beautiful soft banana, not too cold or too hot, or too sweet or too sour, or perhaps she can keep it to eat after the ache has stopped. With all sorrow and worry. E.

P.S. Or will you have some charming cake? I wish that person in front of you wouldn't a) always have her ears outside her cap, b) wear that horrible dress with sham tarpaulin trimming on collar and cuffs.

We were all, I think, apt to cherish each other in times of need, as any small community should and often does. In Old Hall especially, we were a household of not more than about twenty all told, and, separated from the main building as we then were, maintained a strong sense of family identity. But I think the feeling that we were responsible for each other's welfare was pretty widespread throughout the Hall. People have sometimes said that the women's colleges at that time were little more than extended boarding schools, but, in my experience, nothing could be wider of the mark. No cherishing and no freedom had been the way of life at school. At the Hall we were as free and as friendly as we needed to be.

I'm sorry I haven't written sooner but this week I have been busy. There have been all the final schools people to look after. They come in from their papers at about five and we give them tea and supper. I have given two tea parties, one supper party, two Sunday breakfasts and early morning tea for someone very day. Poor things, they are mostly rather depressed.

At the end of my second year I went down for the vac as a woman student and returned in the autumn of 1920 as an undergraduate. Women had at last been granted full university

status (this it may be remarked was years and years before
Cambridge followed suit, in 1946!). There was much excitement and some confusion as to the proper proceeding to be
observed on certain occasions. For instance, all the present
students had to be formally matriculated, and also all past
students who had passed the requisite exams and wished to
take their degrees, were invited to do so. These underwent the
two ceremonies of matriculation and degree-giving in one day,
becoming undergraduates only for a few hours. The university
functionaries were kept very busy. Just before term began, I
had an excited letter from one of my friends who was staying
up at Boars Hill to do some vacation reading.

I have been the first woman ever to sign the University
Register. All of us who happened to be within easy reach
were told to attend so that there wouldn't be such a crowd
when term begins. At the Divinity Schools there were lots of
us and dons and reporters buzzing round. The Beadle led E
and me into the Schools and JB* came over to us. She said,
'As we are the Senior College we sign the register first in
alphabetical order.' The Beadle then took me across the
room and gave me a pen. I saw that the page was blank and
realized that mine was the first signature. The Vice-
Chancellor conducted the ceremony but none of us knew in
the least what to do. He obviously hated the idea of women
being members of the university and sat shuffling his papers
about and frowning. We sat and waited. At last when JB
thought it was time she took me by the hand and led me up
to him and presented me. I said, 'How do you do.' He waved
us aside irritably. 'I'll call you when I want you,' he said, and
at last he did. We stood in a line in front of him and he
presented us with a copy of the statutes and addressed us in
Latin. We hadn't a notion of what would happen next. I
decided 'Hoc volo' would be the thing to say. Then the
Beadle waved us off. When we got out into the quad JB said,

* The Principal

137

'This is the proudest moment of my life and you are historic characters, the first women ever matriculated in the leading university of the world.'

The Principal's sense of achievement and exhilaration was shared by us all, and we donned our new caps and gowns with pride. The gowns were identical with the men's, but the caps had been a matter of serious concern. Ten different shapes were submitted to a Committee which consisted of the Vice-Chancellor, the Proctors, and the five women Principals. LMH was asked to provide two students, one with long hair and one with short to try on each of the ten before the Committee. Our Principal wanted a mortar board, but a softer more comfortable shape was eventually decided upon.

I have ordered my cap and gown, not bad at all. The man in the shop was excited about it all and very kind – showed us B Litt gowns with fur and red edges. 'All ladies', he exclaimed. 'All for ladies!' He was glad to get us before the rush, 30 shillings all together, one just has to choose the size of the cap.

It was splendid for the Principal that in her last year of office (she retired in 1921) there were two events which gave her the greatest possible gratification. Following on the granting of university status to women came the visit of Queen Mary, on whom an honorary degree was conferred. As the senior college we were the first to receive her and Princess Mary accompanied her. We all had careful instructions on how to behave. Everything was to be as informal as possible (of course no elaborate security measures were necessary then). We were instructed that if any one of us were to encounter the royal party on their conducted tour of the college, she must curtsey to the Queen. This filled most of us with embarrassment. I was in one of the common rooms when sounds of an approaching invasion were heard, and we disappeared out of the window just in time. Two students had been deputed to entertain

138

Princess Mary, who asked them to take her on the river. They were just getting a punt untied when a lady-in-waiting came hurrying up to forbid the expedition. We thought this absurd and so did the poor Princess. I suppose they thought we might possibly have upset her.

Another historic occasion during my last year was the Hall Dance. I don't think it could lay claim to being 'a ball' but it was the first ever to which women students were allowed to ask men. It was closed down by the authorities promptly at 11 o'clock, which made us feel foolish, and the refreshments were humble in the extreme, but nonetheless it was a portentious event. I asked a nice boy who was in his first year and had been coached by Mr Tatham. Everyone had to introduce their guests to the Principal who sat in state on high.

Now final schools began to cast their shadow before them and work claimed serious attention. For the first time I started to make some sense of Anglo-Saxon and Old English, for I now had an outstanding tutor in Edith Wardale, another pioneer student of early LMH days. She was small, pale, dry, decisive, and extremely lucid. She inhabited a gloomy flat in Wellington Square and there the cold magic of *Beowulf* and *The Wanderer* began to work on me, though I never came to love them – they were too full of monsters and warriors endlessly 'shaking their spears'.

Far more enticing was the weekly seminar I now had with Prof Raleigh. This was for third year women only and was limited to two or three from each college, so there were only nine or ten of us altogether. Each week someone had to produce and read a paper on a subject of their own choice, which we would then discuss. I did one on 'Poetry for Children' which to my relief Raleigh seemed to like, especially the bits on Charles and Mary Lamb and Jane and Ann Taylor. These last were a lucky hit, for he owned a treasured early edition of them which he afterwards lent me, asserting how much more successful their simple objective poems were with children than the more self-conscious and sophisticated *Child's Garden of Verse* (R L Stevenson) which I had much

139

admired. After these classes some of us repaired to a neighbouring teashop in the High for a riotous meal, and we would walk home together in the dusk full of cream buns and glory.

No-one in my time at Oxford ever thought of going home in term time or of expeditions to London. If I had thought of such a thing I would not have wanted to – it would have seemed pure waste. But before 'Schools' we were all sent off into the neighbouring countryside for 'Schools weekend'. Evelyn and I went to Ashbury on the Berkshire Downs, then a remote and utterly peaceful village smelling of bean flowers. We stayed at the little inn, where we were the only visitors. Behind us a downland track led up to a prehistoric circle in a clump of beeches, and not far away was the famous White Horse, an ancient prancing beast cut in the chalk. My brother had sent me advice for my finals: 'Don't forget to look at the stars', and the near presence of these prehistoric monuments had the same calming effect. I was always happy in chalk country and the weather was fine. We tramped for miles among the flower-laden fields and tried not to think of what awaited us.

It was hot and thundery during my final schools and I had to cope with my usual bugbear of insomnia. After two bad nights, I went to a doctor. Sleeping pills had not been invented but she gave me a bottle of bromide mixture which only made my head feel dizzy. Coming out of the surgery in Holywell I ran into Prof Raleigh who asked me with kind concern if I was ill. 'No,' I said, 'It's only that I can't sleep very well.' He shook his fist at the sky: 'Damn these examinations!' he cried. I felt embarrassed but touched. One day Sally Wordsworth (Miss Wordsworth's niece), who was in her second year and therefore ministering to the third years, gave me a picnic lunch in New College gardens. I remember trying to sleep there under the trees. However, the papers were not too bad and halfway through Miss Spens persuaded me to take the extra paper that was necessary to qualify for a first. The rules for the English School then were that a special subject was obligatory for this. Nominally there was a choice of subjects, but actually there was no choice – it was too much trouble to appoint examiners for a variety of subjects, so almost everyone had to opt for a paper on a very long medieval poem *Sir Gawan and the Green Knight*. I had felt that I was still short of time, the subject did not attract me, and I was not at all ambitious, so I had refused to be bothered with it. Now I agreed to take a sporting chance. One day's gap in my papers allowed me, with help, to prepare three or four passages from the text and to get the drift of the whole. On the appointed morning I found myself sitting next to Ethel. The examination hall was not full and invigilators then must have been less observant or less strict than today, for we exchanged observations on the paper. 'Can you do any? Are you staying?' she asked. 'It's extraordinary. I've got two of the bits I did yesterday, so I'll have a go!' I answered. It would be nice to be able to say that I got my first after this, but that was not so, nor has it made a pennyworth of difference to my life that I missed it. Nor had I expected it. Professor Raleigh admitted to Miss Spens in a letter that in this first year of degrees having been granted to women first classes in English were unofficially rationed to one for each of the women's colleges.

Personally I thought our ration should have gone to Ethel Street. She had, incidentally, a fine way with invigilators. She simply ignored them. Always hard-pressed for time, she would write on and on after the signal had been given for us to stop. Papers were collected, the hall gradually emptied, still she wrote. The baffled invigilator stood helplessly at her desk. 'Really, Miss Street, you must stop now.' 'Yes, yes, in a minute,' she said, tossing yet another page aside. In the end they had literally to drag the sheets from beneath her pen.

My viva was not exacting, most of it consisting of an impassioned argument between the two literature examiners, Raleigh and Quiller Couch, as to which was the better novel – *Emma* or *Pride and Prejudice*. After it was over Evelyn's charming Uncle, Sir Henry Miers, then Vice-Chancellor of Manchester University, refreshed us with ices.

Though I was not at all dissatisfied with my results, the reverse in fact, I was very sad at leaving the Hall. Samuel Johnson says that one tends to forget 'past disadvantages' and that 'recollected attractions blend into a simpler and denser unit of pleasure than ever really existed'. He never said anything that did not contain a measure of truth and of course my time 'up' had contained some difficulties, perplexities, mistakes, and absurdities but emphatically 'the unit of pleasure' *did* exist and was splendidly dense and predominating.

What was to follow was not immediately clear, and meanwhile I went to Normandy with Ethel for a holiday. 'Going abroad' was more of an adventure then, though in some ways both easier and less expensive – no passports necessary and the exchange in our favour. The war had only been over three years and travelling in Europe for pleasure was not the commonplace it has since become. I had not crossed the Channel since childhood and Ethel had never done so. We stayed first in Dieppe with a family (recommended by a French student at LMH) who took in paying guests. Madame was small, brisk, and fierce. She presided over a not too generous table. I can see her now grasping the leg of mutton firmly in one hand while she sliced it into very thin portions with the other. We supplemented our meals with slabs of cheap chocolate.

The most exciting experience of this week at Dieppe was the 'charabanc' rides. Such a way of getting about and seeing the country then was quite new and we found it ravishing. Our driver was an exuberant and gesticulating guide, who paid little attention to the roads which, however, always seemed entirely empty. Norman castles (very romantic for me from childhood because of Charlotte Young's *Little Duke*), Romanesque abbeys, forests, and apple orchards full of happy pigs charmed us on these expeditions, but soon we set off for Rouen. We did not know where to stay at Rouen, so we asked our taximan to take us somewhere not expensive. At first we were enchanted with the ancient house where he landed us, but when a gaunt, unsmiling concierge showed us our vast dark rooms, we felt a bit doubtful. The huge iron beds were covered with soiled quilts; I removed mine gingerly and deposited it in a dim corner. But we thought it clever and adventurous to find ourselves such suitable quarters in this medieval city, with its narrow cobbled streets, open drains, and towering cathedral. That night though, I was afraid of ghosts and Ethel was afraid of being robbed and raped. We stayed three nights in Rouen, entranced by the cathedral, but then we both got ill. The lavatory was also pretty medieval, being a windowless, pitch-dark cabin half way down the steep, winding stairs. We got to know it too well and on the third day we fled and took a lazy river boat to Caudebec.

There was only one little pension at Caudebec then, I think. It was kept by a big, welcoming, blue-bloused man who was a friend of the writer, Hilaire Belloc. He fed us with beautiful omelettes and we soon recovered. We ate these on a balcony overlooking the river with its slow-moving craft. To the right was the 17th-century chateau (now a luxury hotel) and to the left the little town and huge church.

While at Caudebec I made up my mind to go back to Oxford and try to qualify for my degree by taking an intermediate exam. This was a permitted procedure for one year following the granting of university status to women because a number of students, like myself, had not bothered with an intermediate exam as degrees were withheld in any case. A few students were now taking advantage of this dispensation, among them one of my friends, and I now wrote to ask if I could share her rooms in Norham Road. She was taking the History Previous, but this involved two terms so I chose instead an exam consisting of four books of Plato's *Republic* and two books of Herodotus. I had enjoyed what little I had done of Greek and this was a straightforward course, and I thought if I worked hard I could cover it in one term.

The authorities were surprised but amiable about my last-minute plan. 'You are rather a sudden young lady,' said Miss Grier, the new Principal. I liked her. She was ugly but noble, very approachable, a scholar and a discriminating collector of modern pictures. I also liked my landlady and her daughter. Mrs Mackintosh was a Highlander, quarrelsome, generous, funny, and sad. She loved company and was warm towards those of whom she approved. Katharine Briggs, my fellow lodger, and I got on very well with her, though we took care to keep on her right side. It was a lively household: 'Thousands of undergraduates keep on dropping in,' I wrote to my mother.

There were also two married daughters in the near neighbourhood and there had been an adored son who was killed in the war. He was gifted and seems to have been generally much loved. Some lines from a poem of his are engraved round the Edinburgh War Memorial. It appeared that his mother could not forgive Violet, the daughter still at home, for being alive when Alan was dead, for she treated her sometimes with open hostility which worried me greatly. She was a sensitive, clever person with whom I became great friends. She was librarian at the City Library and was a keen politician, a Liberal with an enthusiasm for Lloyd George. She had a romance with a friend of her brother's, but they never liked each other enough at the same time for it to come to a marriage; when he wanted it she didn't, and vice versa.

Katharine and I, who had not before been intimate, though we had liked each other well enough, now became very good companions. We had a little study of our own and used to sit over the hissing gas fire of an evening and exchange confidences. 'Won't it be dreadful if we neither of us ever become famous?' she said one day. I laughed. I didn't think either of us ever would. But I was wrong. Katharine developed into a most eminent Folklorist. She published several very good books, but her great achievement was the editing of the *Folk Lore Dictionary*, a gargantuan task, almost worthy of comparison with Dr Johnson's long labour.* Of all our year she was the one who was to make her mark, but at the time no-one would

* She died in 1982 and there is a Folk Lore lecture established in her honour. Her biography by Ellis Davidson was published in 1987.

have expected this. She had been an unremarkable student, not always popular either with the dons or ourselves. 'Unfortunately I cannot either read Miss Brigg's writing, it is so minute, nor hear her when she reads her essays aloud, she mumbles so,' complained Spennie, and we found her sometimes shy and sometimes overbearing. Now, however, I quickly came to admire her integrity and strength of character and to accept her oddities.

For she lived partly in an imaginary country created initially by her adored father for his children. It was a kingdom similar to the one invented by the Bronte sisters, with a detailed history and geography of its own. Its inhabitants were as real to her as we were, and she would allude to them quite frequently and disturbingly. I had been a little dubious as to how sharing a lodging with her would work out, but quite soon I wrote to Evelyn,

Katharine is so nice, she has only been queer twice. I kissed her goodnight once – quite involuntarily and she blushed but was obviously very pleased, but I did not do it again as I thought she might not always like it. She says she has a sad background to her mind. You know her father, whom she worshipped, died when she was fifteen. She says she has to keep disciplining her thoughts and that was partly why she concerned herself so much with imaginary people – she is frightened of her own thoughts. I understand this well. We are not with each other a lot because of work and being with the family, and so it is perfectly easy to be nice and happy together. She has just given me *Wives and Daughters* by Mrs Gaskell. She hates all modern novels!

Katharine was in some ways a slow developer and found it hard to adjust to the world about her. She and her sisters had been educated by a succession of governesses over whom they seemed to have kept a firm and contemptuous control. They must have been terrors to teach. Katharine alone had experienced a year of boarding school, which she loathed.

Paradoxically, though, she was often rather shy in company and though she was actually humble at heart, she could also be assertive and bossy. This was partly due to the fact that, after her father's death, she became immediately and forever the head of the family. To her mother and sisters her word was law, and she ruled them as a benevolent but indisputable despot. They had a beautiful, remote home in Perthshire, though they were a Yorkshire family, for the father had been an artist with large private means who loved painting mountains and moorlands.

I was awed by the birthday presents Katharine received. What impressed me most was £10 from her mother to spend on books. Even allowing for inflation, the relative cost of books must have been far lower then and all, of course, were hard-backed and well bound and printed.

We went out this afternoon to spend some of K's £10. Think of it! She bought a lovely Oxford edition of Matthew Arnold, a charming Shelley, Peacham's *Complete Gentleman* – that splendid edition. She also insisted on buying me Donne's *Sermons* (Oxford edit) and a lovely Aristophanes for Margaret. That only has spent £2. Since then she has got all the plays of A A Milne and Butcher and Lang's translation of the Odyssey and Bergson's *Laughter*, and she has still heaps more to spend. I was myself tempted to buy four volumes, half calf (1811) volumes of Johnson's *Lives of the Poets* for four shillings the lot. (I have these still).

I found my work hard, though I enjoyed my coachings with Miss McCutcheon, the humourous, encouraging classics don. But I missed the stimulus of essay writing, as all I had to do was to plough through the texts, which I found laborious because there was so much of them and so little time.

In spite of the Mackintoshes and the growing relationship with Katharine, I missed all my other friends greatly and the term as a whole seemed an anticlimax. So I was not sorry when exam time came round again, though I thought I should probably fail. Katharine was very supportive and insisted on sitting on my bed for ages in my icy cold bedroom, wrapped in an eiderdown, so that she could read aloud to me and send me to sleep. This, though it worried me, also touched me and sometimes succeeded, as her voice was low and droning. After my written papers were over I felt very doubtful of my success. However, at my viva I was given a second bit of Herodotus to translate and knew therefore that I still had a chance. The invigilator was most kind. I looked blankly at the paper he placed before me. He bent over me: 'You know,' he whispered 'the bit about the crocodiles'. I did know and it started me off satisfactorily. I enjoyed the rest of my viva. I can't recall the examiners, I'm not sure I ever knew who they were, but we had an interesting discussion on how far Plato can be said to represent the authentic Socrates. I was very glad to have passed for, much as I loved Oxford, I did not want to stay there any longer. These two months had given me an inkling of Greek philosophy and history though I fear knowledge of the language quickly deserted me. It had also given me Katharine as a dear and lasting friend. But it was now time to move on.

CHAPTER NINE

1921–1922
The Settlement

Up in the school room of Northcourt House, in company with the china cats, I pondered over my future. I did not want to read for a further degree, nor did I particularly want to teach – teaching was the most usual profession for women graduates to follow and training was not yet demanded. Of my year at college, two-thirds went straight into a teaching career. And of my intimate friends, six went into teaching, three were 'daughters at home' only three married owing to shortage of men and these three all taught first. Married women teachers were almost unheard of. Evelyn was installed at a private school in Eastbourne, though she and I did have thoughts of starting a nursery school in Abingdon, as we both enjoyed small children.

Miss Spens had suggested WEA lecturing to me. WEA was a recent development in education, really meant for the 'working classes', and the idea attracted but also alarmed me, so I didn't go further than thinking about it. Then I happened to pick up a library book which was lying about on the schoolroom table. It was a life of Canon Barnett by his wife* and there was nothing very extraordinary about it or how it was written – it was just a straightforward account of his experiences, mostly among the London poor – but it was reading that book that made me suddenly decide to do a span at the LMH Settlement in Lambeth.

I knew of the Settlement because the Warden came once

* Henrietta Barnett, a founder of Hampstead Garden Suburb

every term to the Hall to tell us about it. These meetings were not always very well attended. There were some enthusiasts, of course, but in my time their numbers were falling off and more people had to be pressganged to come by appeals to duty and politeness. I had been only mildly interested in these meetings, and now this resolve carried with it no special emotional urge. I thought it might be an interesting experience which could be entered upon without any serious commitment, for in social work, as in many other spheres, far less professionalism was then demanded.

The Settlement movement had sprung up towards the end of the last century. The idea of living actually among 'the poor' and of sharing as much as possible in their lives, while providing help of all kinds for them, appealed to the idealism of a romantic age. Before the advent of the Welfare State, such settlements provided a lifeline in a sea of great poverty.

Our settlement was founded in 1897, inspired by Toynbee Hall, and had a strongly 'Oxford Movement' flavour. The atmosphere was rather that of a religious order – dedicated and devout. The permanent residents in my day were all unmarried women of independent means, whose energies and affections (and often too, their money) were channelled into their work which was their life.

I wrote to the Settlement and arranged to start there in January. My parents were staying with my brother and his wife in Devon where he had bought a practice, and where we had spent Christmas. 'I am more and more in a funk about the Settlement,' I wrote. 'I shall be years and years the youngest there and I should think the most inexperienced and incapable person they have ever had.' I arrived on a dark, cold, dirty day at the old house in Kennington Road, Lambeth. The light over the door shone on the crest of three daisies, chosen for LMH by Miss Wordsworth (and long ago abandoned as being too sentimental). It now seemed to welcome me. So did the Morris wallpaper in the dining room which was the same willow pattern as that in the dining room in Old Hall. Yet, at the same time, these familiar objects made me feel rather forlorn, for I

149

knew no-one here and, outside the windows, instead of the gardens and the river and the chiming Oxford bells, the trams were thundering along the Old Kent Road.

The Settlement owned three adjacent 18th-century houses, tall and narrow, which had connecting passages. I had a big attic bedsitting room at the top of one of these. It belonged to a resident worker who was having a term off, and was sparsely furnished with a high iron bedstead, a table, a small writing desk, a basket chair, and two upright chairs, and was warmed by an antiquated gas fire fitted with a shilling meter. This fire terrified me. It spat and hissed and cursed me whenever I dared to light it. On the walls were some framed photographs of clergymen in groups, and one enlargement of a beaming Bishop. These guardian clergymen in their heavy, dark oak frames, peering down from the embowering, Morris, many-leaved wallpapers, were in every room of the Settlement. There was even one on the inside door of the bathroom – it was a long narrow compartment, so he was at a discreet distance, but I never quite got used to him being there.

The Warden and Sub-warden both belonged to distinguished clerical families, and there was a little chapel at which the Anglican offices were said every day. Attendance was voluntary but expected if work permitted, and I enjoyed the beauty of the liturgy and the peace of the little place, especially in the evenings which I found lonely. Everyone was very kind but no-one was young except one other student who was not resident, and of whom I saw little. There was no social life, as everyone seemed too busy, and people met together only at meals, which were hurried and pretty austere. My days, however, were too full for loneliness.

Much of the Settlement work was for children, and representatives sat on 'Care Committees' in all the local schools. There was also an Apprenticeship Committee which placed promising boys and girls in jobs with good prospects. The Lambeth branch of the Invalid's Children's Aid Association was centred in the Settlement, which had been a pioneer in this field. Two local pubs – the 'Cathedral' and the 'White Horse' – had been acquired for children's clubs.

I found myself immediately and breathlessly involved in all these activities. On my first morning I was set down at a desk by Miss Perkin, who ran the Apprenticeship Committee, and told to deal with that morning's correspondence and to take down the answers. I had never before acted as a secretary and have never done so since, and could not type or spell, but that did not seem to matter. I found working for Miss Perkin the most rewarding, interesting, and hopeful of all my Settlement jobs.

I was soon sent to interview firms and report on their possibilities, and to visit parents and to attend the evening meetings when they came for advice and information. It was cheerful and satisfying work. There was news of apprentices who were doing well, and others who had to be encouraged, financial help to be sorted out, and misfits to be realigned. But, as far as I can remember, there were only a few failures. The chief apprenticeships were in millinery and dressmaking for girls, and for boys coachbuilding, carpentry, furniture making, and printing. Miss Perkin was very efficient and kind, but exceedingly firm with both parents, children, and employers.

The Cathedral, a club for small children, was my weekly Waterloo. I was there when it opened for the first time. It was only a tiny place and, when the door was thrown wide, an engulfing tide of small, shouting, screaming, striving creatures swept in. We could only just manage to shut the door against a further incoming wave, the room being already crowded to bursting, while outside all the mothers of the unsuccessful children battered at the walls and windows so that we had to send for the police to disperse them. After a week or so things quietened down, and enough order was established for organized games to be played and even for stories to be told in a corner to those who wished to listen. I enjoyed doing this. The little girls were quieter, but the boys were more friendly, though demons. I was always utterly exhausted after my Cathedral sessions.

I had to do a good deal of visiting for the Care Committee, and I made friends with some of the mothers. There was Mrs Barton, one of the tragic ones: 'A sad, hopeless visit. Mrs B, very ill with bronchitis and asthma, Nora, her daughter, can't leave her so all our plans for her are postponed. I could do even less for them than before and felt more helpless, it all seemed so hopeless. I wish I could give her some money, but it is strictly against Settlement rules to give money privately. She seems to have lost all her courage and poor little Nora, just turned 14 and delicate enough to need special care, with more trials and anxieties than she can well carry.' (I did however manage later to help a little financially.)

Then there were the happy-go-lucky mothers: 'Mrs J. promised to send her boy round to the clinic after a little pleasant talk. He has sores, bad eyes and general debility. His mother says it's from eating too much liquorice! She says she hasn't time to take him to the Eye Hospital because she had had two babies last week – one on Wednesday and one on Thursday. This seemed rather excessive to me, even for Lambeth, but I realized she must be a 'baby minder'. The passage where we stood talking smelt terribly. We parted, very amicably: "And an awful day it is, makes you regular down about everything, don't it – well, goodbye Miss and thank you. I'll send him along, sure I will."'

And there was Mrs S, clean and animated with her hair in neat curl papers, biting at a piece of coconut all the time she was talking. 'Well, all me daughter's teeth are come out, four together the other day, I dunno why – well I suppose eating this sort of stuff, like me, I ain't one to talk am I, eating this all the while. I'm sorry I can't give you any money today, but I'll send the girl round with 6d on Friday and thank you Miss. I wish you well.'

Then there were the angry ones; 'I'll not have my child hurt, not if I was to go to prison for it – poking and prying here – why half of 'them' hasn't got no children and the other half won't have a chance to have any – I don't mean you, you're young – I mean those who sent you.' She had a most remarkable pair of eyes which so fascinated me I could hardly think of what to say; they were fine, with a capital 'F' and I'd never seen such lashes.

I always found much to admire and to wonder at in the way these women managed to carry on, for the most part cheerfully, and I think I was better at visiting than at trying to organize games at the Cathedral. But the ugliness of the streets and the buildings, and the perpetual smell of stale fried fish oppressed me. The Old Vic was a beacon shining forth among all that sordid grimness. It was then still under the management of Lilian Baylis, that remarkable eccentric who had made it her business in life to bring the people out of the streets into the rehabilitated old music hall, affectionately dubbed, for all time, the Old Vic, and pump them full of Shakespeare. It was possible to buy a seat for sixpence, and I think school parties paid even less. Matinees were crowded out with spellbound children. The audiences were still drawn largely from the locals and on one occasion there was a call for 'author, author', at the close of the performance. There it was possible to see stars in the making. I was about ten years too early for Gielgud and Ashcroft, but I remember Jean Forbes Robertson as a very young Juliet.

The Settlement houses had long, narrow back gardens which were used for all sorts of useful purposes, but there were little or no public open spaces nearby. Bedlam, now the Imperial War Museum, was then surrounded by high walls. I would think of its grim history as I hurried past them. Besides the Old Vic and Bedlam, the only other large buildings near the Settlement were the huge Victorian Gothic church and the Public Baths, of equal size and dominance, and each highly symbolic and significant, rearing their giant bulk among the little mean houses. Victorian architecture had not yet been reinstated as worthy of regard, and I thought these hideous as I had thought North Oxford hideous. The idea of a Victorian Society formed to appreciate and preserve such buildings would have seemed to me amazing, for I despised them as

Thackeray and his comtemporaries had despised the 'plain, dull, ugly' 18th century buildings.

I felt claustrophobic among the endless drab streets, and welcomed the light and space of the river when, on my free afternoons, I crossed Waterloo Bridge into another world. Most of the families I visited had never crossed that bridge. The contrast between the two worlds hit me. I wrote home once: 'I went into the worst street I have ever been in last Wednesday afternoon, and got caught in a storm of wind and rain just where there was no possibility of any shelter I could bear to take. From that street and the misery of it, I went off to have tea in a West End Fullers with an Oxford friend, beautifully dressed and cared for (she was, I mean). What a terribly queer state of things.'

As spring advanced, the ugliness of the street seemed to get worse, but I wrote that 'I have found one bright spot – a sort of flower shop, meant for funerals really and full of wreaths, but they do sell separate flowers and I got some daffodils which now brighten up my room. The shop woman, a cheerful old body, was convinced I wanted these for a wreath and insisted on adding some ivy 'which goes so well in making one up dearie''. So even Oakley St has yielded up some beauty at last.' I was gradually becoming more interested and more useful, especially at the Apprenticeship work. 'Last Friday evening, from 7.30 till 10 pm, a ceaseless stream of people had to be seen. I had to cope with these entirely by myself without advice or consultation. These were quite new applicants which means that all details as to family (each member of it), names, ages, work, wages, rent rooms, insurance, references, employers have to be elicited from parents and school standards, tastes, health, wishes as to type of work, clubs, scouts etc. from the girl or boy, then a full description of the people – how they strike you and any details you may have picked up in the answers have to be written up for each one. I think I got on all right.'

All the same I confess in another letter: 'I have been working really quite hard since I saw you last, but not nearly so hard as most people here, and doing so very little that's any good. In spite of much interest in the people and the desire to help, I don't really *like* the work you know and am always fearfully glad when it is over. But I fear I am like that about most work in varying degrees. Are most people lazy do you think? They *can't* be as lazy as I am.' My admiration and liking for my fellow workers steadily increased and they were so kind and appreciative of my efforts, but I always felt a bit lonely at the Settlement.

While there, I went up to Oxford for a weekend to take my degree and wrote out of a full heart: 'I was fussed over to my heart's content. Why is it that at Oxford immediately, without any effort and absolutely as a matter of course, I become an entirely natural, capable, sensible and delightful person? I mean people *think* I am (and I think so too in a detached kind of way!) So it is rather hard coming back here again where I'm none of these things.'

All the same, when the time came, I was sad to leave the Settlement. I had come to be very fond of the people there and grateful because they seemed to think I had been of help. Miss Perkin of the Apprenticeship Committee even said that, with more experience, I would become a valuable worker, but I knew that this was not what I wanted. In the last letter I wrote from the Settlement I say: 'I can't convey the feelings of kindness I have about me tonight. Miss Gore (Sub-warden) asked me all sorts of questions about what I want to do in the future and Miss Thickness (Warden) may help me to find some coaching, she is going to ask round at several schools. Miss Perkin again thanked me so gratefully for my help. It makes me ashamed of my half-heartedness.'

In the late spring of that year I went with Evelyn for my first visit to Italy. The journey started from Lambeth in a cold black fog and ended in glory. It spread over three days and nights (as we broke it at Paris), and was in itself a supreme adventure. We had sleepers (paid for by our fathers), and the first night I lay in my top bunk too excited to sleep. Hanging round my neck was my money in a little bag (no travellers' cheques then) and under my pillow was *Romola* which I had hoped to read aloud to Evelyn, but she refused to listen as she hated historical novels and in this case I don't blame her. It was a choice between that, *The Ring and the Book*, *A Wanderer in Florence* by E V Lucas, and Tawney's *Acquisitive Society*! Actually I read very little of any of these, but I did keep a short journal of the holiday and began it in the train:

'We have just emerged from Mt Ceni's tunnel and are in Italy at last. It is still grey and cold but there is a bullock cart with bright blue wheels opposite to where we have stopped, and a white southern looking house has a bright blue frieze round it. I have not slept much – perhaps it is the macaroni – such masses of it and I can't keep up to the pace of most people – they must have mouths like rabbits – the most perfect young Frenchman sat opposite us at dinner – he was reading Cicero between courses, turning over the pages with long white soft fingers and polished finger nails. He dusted each plate, knife, fork and spoon before using them and as soon as he had done, put on a pair of pale grey suede gloves. When I slept I had a nightmare that I was an English soldier, very frightened, defending the carriage against Germans who were advancing along the corridor. The second night I slept much better and only woke to hear a magic voice calling 'A Roma, a Roma!' It was at Pisa and it was 4 am – too dark to see the leaning Tower.'

We arrived at Rome soon after ten in the morning. The train was more than one and a half hours late, for my Rome was pre-Mussolini and the trains did as they liked. My Rome was altogether leisurely and peaceful, with the Forum pleasantly untidy and covered with trailing wisteria and little red roses. The whole city seemed to smell of wisteria. There was little traffic except horse-drawn carriages, push bicycles, and the occasional train.

Our hotel, an unassuming and inexpensive one that only provided sleeping accommodation, was situated close to the Borghesi Gardens, in which we used to walk in the cool of the early mornings and evenings. We had most of our meals sitting outside a little cafe watching the street life. 'The children are lovely with beautiful wicked smiles and the peasant women are lovely too – their carts bright blue or red, the wine carts with hoods and bells and their mules always have their dinners of straw tied onto their sides so that in leisured moments they can take a bite.' When I think of the sounds of Rome now, I hear the clatter of little hoofs, and the splashing of fountains and voices and bells.

We were lucky in that both my sister (who was working at the Insitute of Horticulture in Rome) and Evelyn's Uncle Harry, who was staying with a friend, were available for advice, and my journal begins to read like a guidebook, but there are some personal comments and some details that reveal a vanished world.

'In the Sistine Chapel I lay on my back on a bench to see the ceiling properly and took a long time over this.' I do not mention anyone else being there, though, as it was Easter, I can't imagine that Evelyn and I had it to ourselves, but there was certainly no hint of crowds or hurry.

On Easter day we went to St Peter's. 'We drove in one of the little carriages through the Borghesi Gardens past roses and lilac and wisteria and beautiful fresh green oaks and dark masses of pine out along the Tiber, past Hadrian's tomb and so into the huge Piazza San Pietro. Inside the Cathedral, which I found unimpressive except for its size, the vast open space dwarfed the moving crowds. Far away you caught a glimpse of Cardinals and priests and swaying censers. The music made Evelyn feel so bad she had to leave me and wait outside for me. It made her think of all the worst moments in her life, so she said, but then she really seems to hate all music except Gilbert & Sullivan. I moved a little nearer and followed the service for a short time and then joined her outside and we walked right round to the Vatican entrance where there is a little quiet courtyard with a fountain (of course). There we sat and watched the Swiss guards, beautiful people with marvellous clothes designed by Michaelangelo. They were talking and laughing with the tiny beggar children who were playing about round them – I too got a very nice smile from one of them! We then climbed a cobbled path and looked down on the dome and onto an empty courtyard with orange coloured houses and finally walked back through the long, quiet street past the Pope's old palace.' Yesterday the maid called us with 'A good day to you, Christ is dead and it behoveth you to pray.'

Evelyn's benevolent and cheerful Uncle Harry's old friend was a Mr James, with whom he was staying. He lived in Rome and was on good terms with the nobility there. The two of them entertained us one afternoon on the Aventine, the hill the Plebs used to occupy. We had tea at what was once a big Roman farmhouse with a wonderful view over the city. 'Uncle Harry is so nice and not so worryingly scholarly as Mr Tatham, I never feel shy of him. What ages it seems since he treated us to ices at Oxford on the day of our vivas. Mr James, his friend, seems to know everything about everybody. He left us to play on a beautiful Bechstein belonging to a princess whose country home is in a forest which is the haunt of brigands. However, he says the brigands are on quite good terms with her household, play with the children and sometimes take their meals with her servants. When asked how they lived she replied casually, 'Oh from what they can take from people'. Uncle Harry told us that one day he got tired of looking at pictures in the gallery and, happening to have a clockwork mouse in his pocket which he had bought for a child, he wound it up and put it on the floor. Immediately everyone in the gallery, including the attendants, crowded round to look at the mouse, and were transfixed until it stopped. I think this might be a good way, with an accomplice, to steal a picture.'

I was very reluctant to leave Rome, even though I did not want to miss out on Florence, and both time and money were running short. Although I threw a coin into the famous fountain which is said to ensure a return, and though I have visited Italy several times since, I have never been back to Rome. So it remains for me an enchanted city, unravished by the present, dreaming like the Sleeping Beauty amid its twining branches of flowers and its glorious ruins.

Florence I found full of charm but less exciting. If Rome had changed little since the days of Byron and Shelley, Florence was still largely the Florence of the Brownings or perhaps of E M Forster's *Room with a View*. Both our rooms at the Pension White had views. Mine looked out on the Arno and the lovely Trinita bridge (blown up by the Germans in the 1940s and rebuilt after the war), Evelyn's on the lovely Brunelleschi dome and Giotto's tower, 'all one had dreamed of and amazingly newer'. These and Santa Croce and the Fra Angelico frescoes especially entranced me, and I found the side streets and shops intriguing and medieval enough. But I noted that 'there are shopping areas very like Bond Street which you would never find in Rome and altogether it seems busier – possibly because the King of Italy has just been here and he has made everything crowded and noisy with guns and soldiers, most annoying and silly.'

The weather broke suddenly and we spent much of our time in the incomparable picture galleries. I fell in love with Botticelli's Venus and wrote a bad poem to her. I was struck with the impact made by seeing paintings in the original that I had known only from reproductions. 'I had no idea how inadequate and bad copies of pictures can be. Photographs are better but, of course, with photographs you can't have colour.' Evelyn, who was much more knowledgeable about painting than myself, did much to educate me and form my taste. I loved the early Renaissance and the Flemish pictures best (and still do) but I can't yet take Rubens. 'There is a whole Rubens room in the Uffizi – it is a good plan to collect him altogether so that one doesn't come across him with a shock, but can omit him peacefully.'

My birthday was spent at Fiesole. It was our last day and the sun shone again and there were violets out all over the place, just as there were for E M Forster's Lucy, and though I wasn't, like her, kissed among them, I did have a love letter in my pocket that morning.

Actually, for months past I had been trying to make up my
mind upon what was the most important issue of my life and
had by now come to the right decision. Just before I left the
Settlement I had paid a certain visit in Blackheath. Coming
back from this visit, I missed taking two succeeding trains and
one bus (No 48). Waiting at Greenwich Park gates for a second
bus, wet through from walking across the Heath in the pelting
rain, I was oblivious to all delay and discomfort. The bus came
and I climbed to the top and buttoned myself in under the
tarpaulin cover, for it was still raining, but I wanted somehow
to be in the open air.

It takes a true and lasting love to make the Old Kent Road
'blossom like the rose', but it did so blossom for me that day.